P9-BYR-675

TOTAL TEEN

TOTAL TEEN

TRACY ANDERSON'S GUIDE TO HEALTH, HAPPINESS, AND RULING YOUR WORLD

TRACY ANDERSON

RODALE
KiDS

Rodale books may be purchased for business or promotional use or for special sales. For information, please e-mail: BookMarketing@Rodale.com.

Printed in China
Manufactured by RRD Asia 201709

Rodale Inc. makes every effort to use acid-free ♾, recycled paper ♻.

Exercise photographs by Mitch Mandel/Rodale Images

Lifestyle and exercise studio shots by Ryan Olszewski/Rodale Images

Book design by Carol Angstadt and Jan Derevjanik

Library of Congress Cataloging-in-Publication Data is on file with the publisher.

ISBN 978-1-62336-932-3

Distributed to the trade by Macmillan

2 4 6 8 10 9 7 5 3 1   paperback

To my two glorious children
Sam Anderson and Penelope Blythe Mogol

CONTENTS

My story starts out as most stories do, far from the happy ending, but full of hints about what I might achieve if I listened to my inner voice and found my own strengths.

For me, it was always about dance. Decades before I would work with Gwyneth Paltrow, Jennifer Lopez, Lena Dunham, or any "celebrity," I was consumed with my own artistic dream. I desperately wanted to be a professional dancer. My mother gave me the love of movement, the one that I still carry with me today. She was a ballerina and owned a dance studio in our small town in Indiana. From the time I could walk, I was dancing. My mom would blast all kinds of music in our living room and cheer, "Move, move, move!" She would push me to wiggle, twist, shake, and leap in unstructured ways, asking, "How does Tracy want to move?" This empowered me to begin to listen to what my body wanted and to learn to trust my physical self.

In high school, my passion for dance translated naturally into cheerleading, though I was not blessed with the gift of flexibility, a coveted trait in the cheering universe. Some girls could easily tie themselves in twisty knots or land complex back handsprings. I had to work really hard at every part of it.

The summer after high school, my dad saw an ad in the local paper announcing auditions for a Hollywood movie filming in my town. It was a basketball film called *Blue Chips;* I'm pretty sure it's on Netflix if you want to check it out. The casting agents were looking for "real cheerleaders." When I arrived at the audition in my school's official cheer uniform, I was shocked and embarrassed to find the other girls in sexy outfits, in the half shirts and tight biker shorts that were all the rage in 1994. I told my mom that I needed to change immediately, that I had to look like everyone else, but she convinced me to stay in my uniform. This was a moment that I will never forget, when I had to screw up my courage and decide to be myself instead of trying to look or be like the rest of the world.

Amazingly, I made the cut and landed one of the roles. This was my introduction to movie making, but also to fierce competition and ridiculous fad diets. Many of the other actresses on the set were following the trendy "pineapple diet." Something inside me knew that consuming basically nothing but pineapple would be a bad move—though I did feel tempted to try it several times!

I survived my 15 minutes of movie fame and resumed my original ambition to become a professional dancer. I knew I wasn't Juilliard material right out of

the high school gate and wasn't likely to win a spot at the famous New York City arts conservatory. I just didn't have the gifts required to make it into a top school like that, but I still was good enough to pursue dance competitively, and I was an extremely hard worker. Staying focused and driven, I managed to get into a different but still very competitive conservatory, the American Musical and Dramatic Academy in Manhattan, and even win a scholarship. My program required the students to do it all—to act, sing, and dance. Jesse Tyler Ferguson was in my class; Jason Mraz was a friend and at the school at the same time. It's funny that he was in the drama program and is a musical genius. We were at a place to be able to find our way. The school had a lot of talent, and we had to perform at our highest level.

Although I had done only a small bit of acting, the most challenging part for me was the singing. I wasn't born with a natural vocal gift. I almost felt ill at the thought of having to stand up and sing to be critiqued in front of my peers. My roommates could prepare their songs without struggling as I did. To this day, I am still very close with my roommates Tamera, Candice, and Heidi, and they love to remind me how painful it was to listen to me rehearse "Matchmaker" from *Fiddler on the Roof*. However, looking back on my education, I am grateful that I was forced to explore all of the performing arts, not just the areas where I knew I could shine. If nothing else, this teaches you how to give it your all by being out of your comfort zone in safe environments as well as reaffirms your real passion.

Going in, I felt confident about my dancing talent. Dance, specifically ballet, had always been my everything. I clung to it, even as key pieces of my life were unraveling. My parents divorced when I was a senior in high school, and I had never quite regained equilibrium after that. I was super close with both my mom and my dad, and their split was tough for me to process or even accept. When I wasn't busy dancing with my mom, I was playing chess with my dad, who reveled in the game's strict rules and was equally excited when I learned how to break them. No divorce ever comes at a *good* time for a kid, but my parents' timing was particularly awful. I didn't realize it when we were an intact family unit, but their marriage provided a real sense of security for me. When it ended, I lost a lot of my footing; my world was rocked.

This was a terrible way to start college. Here I was, light-years away from my tiny Indiana high school, nose to nose with talented kids from all across the country, being asked to show up in ways I never had before, singing, acting, giving my best as a dancer—and on the inside, I was falling apart, my heart breaking.

On the outside, things were changing, too. Money was extremely tight. My mom had to work three jobs to keep things going for my sisters, brother, and me. She had dropped me off at school in New York with only $20 in my pocket. Whenever I wasn't in class, rehearsing, or performing, I was working odd jobs, first as a waitress at a little Italian restaurant on the Upper West Side, and then as a salesgirl at the Gap on 86th and Broadway. Even so, after tuition and living expenses were paid, I had zero budget for healthy food. I survived on bagels with mustard and tomato, frozen yogurt, and—thinking they must be healthy—fat-free snack foods.

The physical effects of this diet were not subtle. I began to gain weight and was immediately thrust smack back into my insecurities from an angle I had never experienced and one that threatened my passion. I gained 35 pounds in 18 months. This is a disturbing weight gain for anyone, but for someone who's 5 feet tall and determined to be a professional dancer, it's downright devastating. If I had been an accounting or history major, it probably would have been a different story. I could have been fine in a sweater and jeans in the library, hiding behind my books as I worked to combat the weight or just learned to accept my new shape. Instead, my dance curriculum required me to be onstage several times a day, in front of many people, most of them paid to judge my performance. I could feel my instructors clocking, often not so quietly, every pound that found its way to my hips.

Dance, and acting too, are generally realms reserved for the super fit and skinny. It was really painful to see that I was sabotaging my success as a dancer even though I was doing nothing but trying to succeed and make my ballerina mom proud, like any child would. I felt my dream career slipping away from me every time I stepped on the scale. My instructors didn't help my confidence. After class they'd say things like, "If Disney stays on Broadway, you could get character work, maybe as the teapot" or "It's such a shame that you've gained weight, because you have a lot of talent."

So I ate less, letting go of my treasured frozen yogurt, and kept dancing at least 4 hours every day. But I still couldn't seem to shake the majority of the extra weight.

Luckily, wisely, I never turned to drugs and didn't develop an eating disorder, but boy, did I start to overexercise. After dancing all day, I'd take a Pilates or step aerobics class, pushing my body to its limits in the hopes of meeting the unrealistic expectations of the dance community.

I definitely wasn't ready to stop trying. In fact, I was more motivated than ever to get my body back. Now, I just needed to find the right solution to my problem.

A LOVE OF MOVEMENT,
THE BIRTH OF A METHOD

After I graduated, I stayed in New York, got an agent, and landed a few respectable gigs. I was the understudy in a Broadway show and made an equity performance of *A Chorus Line* in Chicago. I certainly showed my college instructors that I could be more than a Disney teapot. But I was still struggling with my weight the entire time. The professional performance world was much worse than the conservatory; we were all competing for the same limited roles, and the vibe was cutthroat.

To stay in the game, I had to be as thin as possible, but I was starting to see that I couldn't manage my weight in a healthy way. My body was not happy living on steamed chicken breast and plain veggies while squeezing in multiple aerobic classes a day and running to audition after audition. This pace was out of balance. I couldn't listen to my body and understand its cravings, messages about what I needed to stay healthy, protect my menstrual cycle, and properly manage my stress before it turned toxic.

I was starting to lose my love for the dancer life, in all its variety. I felt like a failure, a disappointment to my mom and to myself. Every family conversation revolved around my career, not around my happiness and health. My parents wanted for me only what I appeared to want for myself, but I was hiding the truth about my personal journey. I didn't tell them that I had lost touch with joy and needed a reality check.

My boyfriend at the time was Eric Anderson, who was a professional basketball player for the New York Knicks. He is 6 feet 8 inches tall; I always found it funny when he towered over me. We had met during the filming of *Blue Chips* in Indiana and had been dating off and on ever since. He had seen me through years of weight struggles and had always supported me through disheartening times. We eventually got engaged, a happy moment despite my inner troubles.

At this point, my efforts to break into the dance scene in NYC just weren't working. My agent sent me to LA on acting auditions, but all I wanted to do was be a dancer. My dreams hadn't changed, although I still couldn't seem to keep my weight down. Eric and I started our life together as an engaged couple. I was on the brink of giving up altogether when I found out that I was pregnant with my son Sam. Around the same time, Eric injured his back and was sent to a summer rehab program for hurt players. I went with him and met a doctor who would unknowingly plant the seed that would blossom into the work that I do today.

This passionate doctor, a huge basketball fan, was doing a research project to see if there was a way to optimize a method of muscular training for basketball players to protect their spines to prevent future back surgeries or to help them return to top physical form without needing major surgical intervention. The doctor had seen many players end their basketball careers prematurely and end up in La-Z-Boys for the rest of their lives.

The doctor had done extensive muscle biopsies to study the strength and flexibility of muscle tissue. He wanted to understand how the brain participates and how to create strength that was strong yet flexible enough to allow the athlete to perform fast and injury-free. How could players perform at a professional level yet still remain healthy? What exact movements would keep the muscles perfectly in balance? The doctor was attempting to discover which rehabilitation exercises could maintain the positive effects of back surgery or prevent it altogether.

This is where I came in! Basketball isn't dance, but being a top athlete involves a level of choreography; you have to do a series of orchestrated movements to get to an end result. I could do that. Out of curiosity, and purely to help Eric's back heal, I asked the doctor to talk to me about what he was doing, and he quickly saw that I had a knack for understanding his project and its goals. I was clearly passionate about how bodies moved and knew a lot about how they worked. After helping him come up with initial movement concepts for a preventive program for basketball players' backs, I wondered if it would be possible to develop a series of movements for any part of the body. And if I could do it for a basketball player, could I do it for a dancer like myself? I was suddenly determined to create a program that would help dancers reach their optimal form.

I didn't want to wing it. I did research and conducted studies. I learned everything I could about the connection between the brain and the body, and the way that our bodies can morph given the right circumstances, revealing what's truly possible and connecting back to our primal selves. I applied everything I learned to myself and realized, "This really works!"

I engaged with 150 different women and measured them for 5 years in 20 different areas as they worked with me to become as strong, balanced, and healthy as possible. At the beginning, each of them was lacking balance and self-confidence, and many even felt deeply disconnected from their bodies, as if they were resigned to their fate based on their genes, or their metabolism, or whatever else it was that made them believe that they couldn't change. They all wanted their bodies to be wildly different from what they were, and this lack of self-acceptance was wreaking havoc on their self-esteem. Their happiness was in some ways directly connected to their weight, and they each struggled to make positive changes. I knew then that my new endeavor was really important and could be for more than dancers alone. I kept researching, kept talking to medical experts, and kept working with women, and soon my mission crystallized: I would develop tools to help create balance where there is imbalance in the body, for everybody and anybody, everywhere and anywhere.

WORD TRAVELS FAST

I was 3 years into my project, working with my first test group in Indiana, when a writer for the *American Idol* magazine called me for a quote. I had helped one woman in particular transform her body beyond her wildest dreams, and people wanted to know how she did it. From there, things got crazy pretty fast. I opened my first studio in California. The clients who came regularly and followed my method noticed their bodies changing, dramatically. Because this was Los Angeles, many of those folks were celebrities. Gwyneth Paltrow heard about me through a friend and asked me to please help her lose weight after the birth of her son, Moses. After she left our first appointment, she called her friend Madonna, who had recently been recovering from a horse riding accident. You can guess how it went from there.

The funny thing is that I never set out to build a business or a brand. I was really only interested in each person who stood in front of me, and in creating a program that was customized to their unique body type, fitness level, and lifestyle. I was a farm girl from Indiana, but now the paparazzi were circling around me! I was called a "secret weapon" for celebrities and an "exercise guru." I was portrayed as a ruthless trainer who demanded that her clients work out 2 hours a day, 6 or 7 days a week, with the goal of achieving a teeny, tiny physique. The truth is that I didn't even know how to explain exactly what I did with my clients. I developed different programs for different people. And I believed then, and still believe now, that teeny, tiny is far from the only way to be beautiful. Feeling connected and in proportion makes everyone feel like they are balancing their mind and body successfully, and owning their choices.

Gwyneth encouraged me to share my work with the world. Hesitant as to how I could share it all but trusting her, I created a series of DVDs. It was really important to me to showcase my method in the right way. I wanted women to understand that restoring balance where there is imbalance—and excess weight is often a sign of imbalance—is a very personal journey. It was impossible for me to summarize my program in a quick interview; you weren't going to get the gist of what I was offering in a 2-minute clip on *Entertainment Tonight*. To make sure that I was really sharing the best of what I had to offer, I knew I would have to continuously produce videos to counteract the message being portrayed that you could get Gwyneth Paltrow's body in a DVD. I created a new program for Gwyneth every 10 workouts, so I needed to figure out how to give everyone else the same opportunity. Many years later I finally created a 4-year-long customized in-home journey in video format called *Metamorphosis* that featured 11,690 movements for the first 90 days; the program is capable of improving any part of your body that has always been a source of struggle. Whatever your genetic weakness, whatever you were born with, like your grandma's thighs, you don't necessarily have to accept it. My method targets all of the body, and all of our bodies.

Women seemed to really like what I was offering, and the results and positive response continue to grow. Today I have seven studios and am in the process of opening more.

YOU'RE AHEAD OF THE CURVE

I've been working with women for almost 2 decades. Everyone has a unique body and a unique take on fitness, but we all have the same goal: to feel good in our skin. And my goal is the same, too. I want to help every person, young and old, restore balance where balance has been lost. If you're overweight, depressed, sleepy, moody, breaking out, or struggling in school, there is likely an imbalance in your body, mind, or emotions; something is off. With simple shifts in the way you eat, the way you move, the way you think, and the way you rest, you can find that sweet spot of equilibrium once again. A healthy life is all about being aware of and reestablishing this balance over and over again, and it's a lot easier to get back to feeling good when you have acquired the necessary tools at a young age.

The adult women I work with spend a lot of time untying the knots of their bad habits. They've been eating the same unhealthy junk foods for so long that their tastebuds go into shock when offered a clean, whole food like a carrot or an apple. They've been combating their afternoon fatigue with so many lattes and double chocolate brownies that they can't imagine their sleepiness may be coming from lack of exercise and sugar crashes.

Adults also struggle with appreciating who they are. So many women want to look like other women and walk me through their celebrity body part wish lists: "I want so and so's abs, so and so's upper arms." I tell them that even though I work with Gwyneth, who's 5-foot-10 with a slender build, I also work with many different women of all different heights and sizes. I work with Jennifer Lopez, who has the sexiest curves on the planet, and the beautiful Lena Dunham, who has no desire to look like a waif. I am interested only in connecting them and balancing them in their own physical self. It is important to know that women are both curvy and slender in different, but awesome, ways. These women also want to feel strong and alert and alive, but they don't want to zap their curves completely or push their bodies into a shape that isn't naturally theirs. This makes me so happy! I love how different we all are, and I am thrilled when I see women click into what makes them special. I get especially excited when I see young girls feeling comfortable in their own skin, appreciating their bodies for all that they can do. The point is that they all wish to be healthy, and they all work at being healthy and aware. You have the opportunity in this book to own the healthiest version of yourself and never lose the incredible and unique you. Part of being healthy and balanced is knowing who you are and loving it.

This doesn't mean that you have to accept your body exactly as it is. If you understand what your body is capable of doing naturally and are empowered with the tools and techniques to enhance its performance, you will be amazed at how good you can look and feel, and how powerfully you can show up for every aspect of your life. All you need to do is listen to what your body is telling you. This is one of the best parts of being a teenager! If you begin now, you'll have a head start that will be with you for the rest of your life.

THIS BOOK IS YOURS! ♡

This book is not about calorie counting or fierce workout routines. There will be no pineapple diets (I learned that lesson a long time ago!) or 2 hours of cardio, 7 days a week. Not here. Creating balance means making all kinds of healthy choices all day, every day, and that includes treats, relaxation, and fun. I see it like this: When you wake up each morning, you are facing about 16 hours of decisions for your body, mind, and spirit. Every drop of food or drink that you put into your mouth is a choice. The way you move—or don't move—your body is a choice. And all day long, the different aspects of yourself are struggling to be heard. Your emotional self is the most relentless and may be yelling at you to stay inside and eat an entire pint of mint chocolate chip ice cream because you're PMSing. But when you do, your physical self and intellectual self suddenly have a lot to say about it; you're bloated from the dairy and jittery from the sugar. By listening to your body's true messages, you can make a better choice the next time your emotions get pushy. (You'll have lots of chances, because they're usually pushy.)

You're in conversation with these various parts of yourself all day long. The more you hone your listening and inner collaborating skills, tuning into what part of yourself needs to win right now, the easier it will be to make decisions that keep you in balance and operating at a top level in all areas of your life: at school, in your extracurricular activities, and with your friends and family. It is actually fun to be a consistent person who is in control. This deep listening is the heart of healthy, balanced living and what I hope you'll take with you from this book. I would never attempt to tell you what is right for you. Only you know what is right for you. But I can share with you the tools that will help you increase your ability to hear what you really need in any given moment. (You may not *really* need a stack of pancakes and a chocolate milkshake, but then again, you might.) Listen closely so that you can make the most balanced choices for yourself.

There is no right way to use this book. You can read it from beginning to end, or you can pick one section, dive into it, and then move on to another. This is *your* book to be used your way. Inside, you'll find three sections: CONNECT, EAT, and MOVE. Each one is full of simple ideas and practices to spark new ways of thinking and new ways of being. You'll find some of my favorite tasty recipes that are easy to make at home, as well as easy breakdowns of movements that will ignite your muscles and clear your mind.

When approaching the exercises, please understand that you are free to move at your own pace. Explore the movements and work up to a max of 40 reps on each side for any given movement. It takes time to "blueprint" the movements. Depending on where you are starting from, you might only want to try one or two repetitions of a movement. You might even feel comfortable trying only a portion of a movement. What matters is that you continue to try and with each try make progress.

In a world where you're bombarded daily with filtered social media images and magazine covers of photo-shopped celebrities, it's essential now, more than ever, to create a rock-solid relationship with what's real and what's beautiful. You are real. You are beautiful. You are enough.

I'm so excited to be your guide as you fortify yourself with the tools to bring out your best—physically, mentally, and emotionally.

With love, and in balance,
Tracy

CONNECT

SECTION 1

I love the human body. I'm continually fascinated by how the body responds to how you treat it, the food you feed it, the way you move it, and the way you mentally digest how you feel as you activate its physical potential. One of the most difficult parts of my job is re-instilling the physical connection that adults have lost with their bodies. They have spent too many years judging themselves and have forgotten how to take any joy from their own strength and grace.

When we are toddlers, we are physically so free, so ignorant of self-criticism. We move, driven by adrenaline and curiosity. We don't create roadblocks for ourselves when we want to be active. If music starts to play, we wiggle, giggle, and rock it out.

It isn't until our parents turn off the music, forget to kick a ball in our direction, or overuse the television to keep us occupied that we fall away from this happy habit of movement. When we tumble and no one encourages us to get up, when we run and someone calls us a slowpoke, when we dance and someone laughs at our missed rhythm, that is when our motivation to move begins to decrease and our physical self weakens in deference to our emotions. We no longer feel like moving, but losing that connection to the needs of our body is the worst thing that we can do to ourselves.

If you want to achieve your goals, both those for your mind and those for your body, you can't tune out your awareness of your physical self. You have to be physically available; you have to hear your inner voice, the one telling you what your body wants and needs. Your mind and your spirit can't be separated from the body that houses them—the muscles, ligaments, bones, and organs all working together in complex ways. Empowering your physical self empowers your heart and brain, too.

Every one of us is a snowflake, pretty similar at first glance, but on closer examination really incredibly different from one another and unique in a multitude of ways. We may be tall or short; have a fast or a slow metabolism that either promotes or challenges our ability to gain or lose weight; have brown, black, red, blonde, or no hair; have green, blue, or brown eyes that see or don't see well—all of us are given a physical self that we did not choose. Not one, in its entirety, is better or worse than any other. But every one of us should feel the best we can in our own body, the one we were born with. Remember, we all have our own given set of physical, mental, and emotional circumstances. It is what we do with them that matters: how we connect to what we are given. How we allow or forbid others to influence our personal decisions about what we want for ourselves.

What is really cool is that we can do a lot with our bodies, if we want to do so. No one else has the right to tell you to dye your hair, wear colored contacts, or lose or gain muscle or weight. It is vital that you learn to listen to your inner voice and decide who you are. Honor your individuality; be courageous for yourself. The more that you connect to yourself, the less you will care about what others think about you and the more you will be able to be in control of your health.

You could say that my entire career has been built on the body, studying what it can do, encouraging it to get stronger and faster, and teaching people how to tap into its power. One of the fascinating things about our muscular structure is that we have the ability to change our muscles, to transform them to match our goals for ourselves. I am 5 feet tall. I don't need the overdeveloped strength of a linebacker. I won't ever be a football player, and I don't want to be. I do want to be lean and strong, and in proportion to my height; I still do want the body of a dancer. If you have a passion for a certain physical activity and put in the work, your body will condition itself to the needs of that pursuit. If you are committed to a sport and put in the hours necessary to do it well, your body will adapt to give you success. The physiques of a swimmer, or a cyclist, or a runner, or a gymnast will all be different. I love how swimmers have broad shoulders and highly defined obliques and how cyclists have super-strong quads. I love yogis' flexibility and dancers' long, strong musculature.

Over the past 15 years I have worked with so many women who are desperately hoping to feel better in their bodies. Some have been struggling with their weight for decades and are exhausted from waging battles with specific body parts, constantly fighting their upper arms, belly, or thighs. They're depleted from comparing themselves to the shapes of others and from scolding themselves: "I should be thinner," "I should be able to fit in those pants," "I should be in better shape." These women will do almost anything to change their bodies and are prepared to sweat, eat nothing but alfalfa sprouts, and exercise for 2 hours a day, 7 days a week. They wait for me to present the fitness routines, the food plan, and the solution that will take them away from the pain they are feeling. Instead, I share what I have learned from all these years of working closely with women and from my own experience with weight loss as a teen: Looking good on the outside must start with feeling good on the inside, as an individual making choices for herself.

I like to think of the body as a house that contains the wonder that is really you. You may think that your body is where you start and end, but trust me, it is only the beginning. You look in the mirror and see that you have brown eyes and curly hair, or blue eyes and straight hair. You may appreciate your cheekbones and be in your own battle with your upper arms, but all of that is far from who you really are. The true essence of who you are doesn't have anything to do with what's on the outside. The real you is your generosity, kindness, intelligence, and humor—the invisible, magical, powerful aspects that make up the total package of you. The real you is all the things that make you happy: your favorite hobbies, the foods you love to eat, your favorite colors, your best friends. The real you is also about the parts of yourself that aren't as shiny: the places where you are sad, lonely, confused, or afraid. A human being is a dynamic combination of the bright parts and the dark and shadowy. Though it doesn't feel like it when you're gripped by heartache, disappointment, or fear, the dark and the light actually work together in a delicate balance of opposing forces. You can't experience joy without sometimes experiencing sorrow. The same goes for success and failure, calm and anxiety, and bliss and pain.

Who you really are is also about what you really love to do. Every single person on Earth has unique desires, skills, and abilities, and a unique purpose that he or she is meant to pursue. One of the best parts about growing up is discovering what you really love to do and how you'll do it—and knowing that nobody will do it exactly like you will.

This doesn't mean you disregard your body. On the contrary! Your body is the vessel that allows your light to shine through. It may sound silly because it's so obvious, but you need your body to do the things you want to do. Your body takes you where you want to go, from school, to swim practice, to that awesome party on Friday night. It's the vehicle that allows you to pursue your dreams and live your purpose, and it's also the way you experience the world.

You've probably heard the expression, "Your body is your temple." It's your temple; it's your sweet little apartment; it's your 30-room mansion with a five-car garage. However you want to look at it, your physical self is an essential part of living a vibrant, joyful life. You can be the most intelligent, creative person in the world, but if you're not feeling good in your body, you won't be able to do all that you hope to do. I like to think of caring for my body the way I care for my home. I know that it's hard to feel safe, relaxed, and comfortable in a home that's messy, dirty, or crumbling from neglect. This is why I keep my house clean and organized, free from dirt, dust, and mold. I also know that it's difficult to feel strong, inspired, and happy in a body that's not being cared for properly. Healthy food, lots of water, consistent sleep, and exercise all help to keep your body functioning at top level. The more you take care of your body, the more the real you can shine through.

THE THREE PARTS OF YOU: WHO'S SPEAKING NOW?

Once you have clicked into the real you and are simultaneously caring for your body regularly, you'll be in a prime position to listen to what you need at different points in time. It's this listening that we're after and that will help you make choices that will lead you to the best and most balanced life yet. Part of honing your listening will be recognizing what part of you is calling out for attention, and discerning a real need from a passing desire. I want you to be empowered with the ability to know what you need every minute of every day. This will help you much more than any set diet I could create or any strict exercise regimen that isn't tailored to your unique self—though in the chapters that follow, I have lots of fun and simple suggestions for healthy, delicious ways to eat (see EAT starting on page 21) and have created a series of movements specifically for teens that will activate and strengthen your body (see MOVE starting on page 43).

In any given moment you will be fielding requests from three distinct aspects of yourself. You can picture them like three overly excited kindergartners vying for their teacher's attention. Each one is waving its hand in the air shouting, "Pick me! Pick me! Pick me!" And, like individual kids, each aspect has its own needs, challenges, and slyly manipulative ways of getting you to do what it wants. Sometimes two aspects will even team up to confuse you so you don't know which part of yourself is actually speaking the loudest! The better you understand how each aspect functions, the easier it will be to manage their needs and live a balanced life.

Let's take a close look at each of them.

YOUR PHYSICAL SELF: NOBODY KNOWS YOUR BODY LIKE YOU DO

Your physical self starts and ends with your body. In that sense it's the most straightforward of all of the aspects of you. Your body's needs are relegated to what it takes to keep all of its systems chugging along without a glitch.

Earlier, we talked about viewing your body as the house that the real you inhabits, but you could also compare it to a vehicle that must be maintained to operate at peak performance. To keep a car functioning at its best, you've got to attend to it on multiple levels; you've got to change the oil regularly, keep the tires full of air, and keep the fluid levels up. Most vehicles are equipped with a clever system of signs that alert you when something isn't optimal. A bright orange light flashes if the tires need air, the brakes squeak if they need fluid, and the oil light flickers on when it's time for a change. Likewise, your body also tells you when it needs something. You just have to learn to recognize its signals.

A car will sputter, slow to a crawl, and then finally stop in the middle of the road if it doesn't have enough fuel. Your body will too, but your physical self takes it a bit further. It doesn't simply require fuel in the form of food; it requires *good* food. That means whole foods, and a variety of them, in the form of veggies and fruits, grains, and lean proteins. If your daily diet consists of Pop-Tarts, pizza, soda, and lattes, your body is eventually going to respond to this insufficient regimen. It will tell you how it feels about being overwhelmed with refined sugar, white flour, and saturated fats—and being denied vegetables and water.

You may end up sluggish or depressed. Or you may find that your skin is constantly breaking out and your belly is often bloated. These are all ways that your physical self screams for help, alerting you to the fact that something is out of balance. The longer you ignore its cries, the worse your symptoms will get. But sometimes your body will speak in a voice that's much softer. These messages are just as important. If you find that you have a low hum of a headache at the end of the school day, you may be dehydrated. If you're having a tough time concentrating during your first class, you may not have slept long enough the night before. If you're grumpy or irritable more often than not, you may be experiencing mood swings from sugar crashes. I want you to be able to hear these whispers, too.

As you first start listening to your body, you will embark on a process of trial and error as you work to discern what's really being said. It's like learning a new language; there is some inevitable guesswork that will have to be done while you get better at translation. Maybe you omit a group of foods from your diet for a few weeks to see if your bloating subsides or if your skin clears up. Dairy, sugar, and refined flour (found in white bread and pasta and all processed baked goods) are often good categories to start eliminating when investigating the cause of a certain symptom. Or you may decide to give yourself an extra hour of sleep each night or up your hydration by drinking more water each day.

The changes you make as you listen to your body can be small, like taking a few minutes to eat a healthy breakfast when you usually start the day with nothing but a cup of coffee or—gasp!—a diet soda. (Don't worry; I've got lots of easy on-the-go breakfast options for you in the EAT section.) Or you may choose to take a walk or practice some of the MOVE exercises in this book instead of keeping it lazy on the couch. Any positive changes that you make will ripple out in beneficial waves. Your increased effort to listen, and respond, to your body sends a big message to your physical self. You're saying, "Body, I hear you. I'm listening. We're in this together." When you make the effort to show up for your body, your body will show up for you.

BRAIN VERSUS MIND

The mind is different from the brain even though they are housed in the same area of the body. The brain is the actual organ, housed in your skull, that serves as the mission control director of your whole physical body. The brain takes in massive amounts of information throughout each day and processes it so you can problem solve and make decisions. The brain also keeps every aspect of your body functioning. When your stomach is full after you've eaten a good meal, it signals your brain to tell you to stop eating. When you want to jump or run or sit, your brain tells your body how to move.

MIND YOURSELF: TUNING IN TO YOUR MENTAL SELF

Once you're empowered with the ability to hear what your body is saying, you'll be well equipped to tune in to the other aspects of yourself. Next up: your mind. Your mind, that invisible realm of your ideas, emotions, beliefs, and imagination, dictates how you see the world. Each thought that sparks and then fades away is born from the mind. Your feelings about the people in your life, your favorite colors, foods, and school subjects are all mind-stuff. The mind is often a very busy place, like a huge train station at rush hour. Hopes, opinions, and judgments all come barreling in and out of the station. Sometimes things get really crowded in there, especially as your life gets fuller and more demanding. In any given moment you could be juggling stress about a major test that you have next week, interest in that cute guy in your geometry class, wonder about what's for dinner, plans for your outfit for tomorrow, worry about global warming, or anxiety about a fight you had with your sister that morning. All these impressions come rushing in and demand your attention. Too much action in the station can overwhelm anyone.

Tuning in to your mind's needs takes a different kind of listening than responding to your body's demands. While your body has clear physiological requirements (food, water, rest) and can get kicked out of balance with too much or too little of anything (too many Doritos, too few carrots, too much chocolate, not enough broccoli), the mind has a different set of guidelines that keep it functioning at its best.

First things first: What does a "mind at its best" look like? It takes a little bit of practice to discern how your mind is feeling in any given moment, but you'll soon get it. The ideal state of mind is calm, clear, and alert. If you are feeling nervous, worried, anxious, confused, stressed, or overwhelmed, your mind is trying to communicate something to you. Luckily, you can begin to understand what it's trying to say—and defuse the bomb that feels like it's about to blow up in your head—with a couple of simple steps.

STEP 1: Notice your thoughts.

Your thoughts are blips of energy that shoot across your mindscape for pretty much every moment that you are awake—think of that busy train station. Most of your thoughts happen unconsciously, rolling through your mind all day long. It takes intention and awareness to notice them. When you're happy and relaxed, your thoughts move in an easy, peaceful manner. They come in and they go out. But when you're feeling worried or stressed, the same thought loops around and around again (*I'm never going to pass tomorrow's test. I'm never going to pass tomorrow's test. Even if I start studying now, I'm never going to pass tomorrow's test*). It's hard to avoid the feeling of being crushed under the thoughts piling on top of each other in a teetering tower of to-dos that quickly seems insurmountable (*I have to study for tomorrow's test and I have to write that paper for English class and I have to go to field hockey practice and I have to figure out who I'm going to invite to my birthday party and I have to, I have to, I have to*). Noticing the content of your thoughts and the way in which they travel through your mind (looping? towering?) is the first step to moving back into a state of calm and relaxation, the only state that allows us to actually accomplish anything.

STEP 2: Breathe.

Crazy as it sounds, the breath is directly connected to your state of mind. Researchers who study conscious breathing and meditation—the practice of using the breath to calm the mind—have found that the way we breathe influences how we feel. Seriously. It's like we all have this gauge inside of us that controls whether we are freaked out or calm and centered. Deep, conscious breaths (actively taking slow, deliberate inhalations and exhalations) soothe your nervous system and signal your thoughts to stop looping and your heart to stop racing. The stress and anxiety you experience when your mind has become dizzy with unhelpful thoughts begin to dissolve when you breathe slowly and with intention.

WHAT'S IN YOUR HEAD? KEEP A THOUGHT INVENTORY

It's a good idea to start keeping a general inventory of your thoughts. You can keep a small notebook with you to jot them down throughout the day. Whenever you catch yourself drifting away from what you're doing in the moment—daydreaming during history class, floating away while cleaning your room—note what you're thinking about and add it to the list. Before you go to sleep each night, take a look at what you've written. What kind of thoughts did you think today? Are there lots of judgments, worries, or complaints?

On the other side, the intensity of difficult feelings increases when you hold your breath or when your breathing is quick and shallow. Think about how you breathe when you're frightened: Your breaths are short and shallow. Or you may even hold your breath. Holding your breath is like pressing the accelerator on a challenging emotion; it makes it bigger and faster!

Mucho Mindful

You may have heard the word *mindful* tossed around by your hippie next-door neighbor or Oprah or a number of other spiritually minded folks, but what does it really mean? And, more important, why should you care? You should care because mindfulness is a quick route to relief. If you're feeling jittery, nervous, worried, fearful, or overwhelmed, activating mindfulness can help to bring you out of the challenging experience and into the present moment, where things are a whole lot easier.

When you're mindful, you are fully engaged in whatever it is that you're doing—studying for an algebra test, giving yourself a mani-pedi, or Facetiming with your grandma. We mostly move through life disconnected from what we're doing in the present moment. Think of brushing your teeth, something you probably do at least two times a day. You may be moving your toothbrush back and forth across your enamel, but while you're doing so, your mind is a million miles away from the act. You're thinking about how late you're going to be for school, stressing about that lab report you haven't yet finished, or replaying the hilarious conversation you had with your best friend last night (the reason why you didn't finish that lab report). If you bring your attention to brushing your teeth instead of doing it on autopilot, you'll activate mindfulness and zap yourself back into the present moment.

The present moment is the best place to be because it's the only place that's actually real. The past has already happened, and the future isn't here yet. Every thought you have is either a recollection of something that has already happened in the past (the past includes last year, yesterday, this morning, and a minute ago) or a guess about what may or may not happen in the future (1 second from now, tomorrow, next week, next year, and beyond). Sure, you may think you're going to bomb the oral report you have to give in Spanish class later today, but you don't really know until it happens. You can't really know anything until it happens. Most of the hard feelings you experience are there because you're busy living in the past (regretting something that happened, feeling guilty or sorry about something that happened, longing for someone or something that isn't in your life anymore) or the future (worrying about something that has yet to happen).

How do you remain in the present moment and mindfully do whatever it is you're doing instead of drifting off into a sea of thoughts? You use your senses (tasting, feeling, hearing, seeing, and smelling) to pay attention to the actual experience of brushing your teeth (or making scrambled eggs or listening to your best friend tell the same story *again*). Give it a try! The next time you start brushing, really feel the toothbrush in your hand and the bristles against your gums, and taste the toothpaste as it moves across your tongue (is it extra minty? cinnamon-y?). Feel the cool water swish from cheek to cheek as you rinse your mouth, and then run your tongue over your sparkly clean teeth. This is mindfulness! You can practice it all day, every day.

Any time you find yourself drifting off into regret about something in the past or worrying about something in the future, bring yourself back to what you're doing in the present moment. You may be sitting on the bus on the way to school (feel the engine rumbling, see the trees passing by through the window, hear the other kids talking and laughing), or running down the field during soccer practice (feel your heart beating in your chest, hear your breath coming in and out of your nose and lungs, smell the freshly cut grass), or typing a paper on your computer (see the words moving across the screen, feel the keys under each fingertip). When you're mindful, you're fully engaged in the present moment. In the present moment it is almost impossible to be anxious or overwhelmed.

> If you are depressed, you are living in the past. If you are anxious, you are living in the future. If you are at peace, you are living in the present.
>
> —Lao Tzu

What You Think, You Become

Once you start paying attention to your thoughts, you may start to notice some patterns. Like most human beings, you'll probably find that the majority of your thoughts have a complaining quality to them. Seriously, check it out. Notice how many of your thoughts are negative observations (*this room is too cold; the teacher is talking too loudly; my pants are too tight; this soup is too salty*) or harsh judgments or comparisons about yourself or others (*Joey has a terrible haircut; I wish my thighs were smaller; I'm not smart enough for this calculus class; Jenny has more style/a nicer nose/more friends than me*). It can be pretty alarming when you

CHALLENGE: A COMPLAINT-FREE DAY

Tomorrow, challenge yourself to have a complaint-free day. Every time a negative thought comes into your mind, simply catch it, say *no thanks,* and find a positive alternative. If you hate riding the bus to school because it's always drafty and the kids who sit in the back are rowdy, focus on something else instead. Tell yourself that getting a ride to school is much better than walking, or remind yourself that taking the bus always gets you to your first class on time. It's not necessary to exaggerate. You don't have to convince yourself that riding the bus is *amazing,* because that just isn't true. But simply finding, and fixating on, a more positive thought will begin to change your experience of riding the bus. Practice this for 1 full day every time a complaint pops into your mind.

see just how much mental energy you're giving to negative stuff. You're not alone. Until they bring awareness to their thoughts, most people spend the bulk of their conscious hours forming silent but cruel opinions. I used to spend so much time creating endless lists of things I wished were different or better, quietly trashing my friends, my clothes, my body, and my boyfriend.

Putting a stop to this negative thought parade is essential for one key reason: Your thoughts become your reality. When you think something negative, you feel pretty awful, and when you feel awful, life is pretty awful. It's a simple equation: $a \rightarrow b \rightarrow c$. Don't believe me? Try it out. The next time you catch yourself judging yourself and others, pay attention to how it makes you feel.

There's no way you can be happy, joyful, or peaceful when you're consumed with mean thoughts. It's actually impossible. And the more you think something negative about yourself, the closer it comes to becoming a reality. Mia Hamm didn't become one of the world's best soccer players by telling herself that she sucks at soccer. Beyoncé doesn't sell out stadiums by telling herself that she can't sing. Rupi Kaur didn't create a bestseller by telling herself that she can't write. On the contrary, high achievers fill their minds with bright and uplifting mantras about who they are and what they can accomplish. They say to themselves: *I'm going to kill it out there today; I'm going to make a lot of people happy tonight; I'm so happy I get to do what I love.*

These kind of affirmations work for regular people, too! See what happens if you start your day with something like, *I'm going to have the best day* or *I'm going to ace my French exam* or *We're going to win our game.* You can aim for something momentous (*I'm going to get that scholarship*) or keep it smaller (*Mom and I are going to get along today*). Before you even get out of bed, say the words a few times out loud or silently. There is no right way to phrase your affirmation as long as it is clear and contains no negatives: *I will ace my French exam* versus *I am not going to fail my French exam.* It may feel silly or forced at first, but the more you do it (and do it with intention), the easier it will be to actually believe it—and when you believe it, things start to shift. It's a guaranteed equation that can be applied to anything in your life, at any time of day.

GETTIN' EMO: IN CONVERSATION WITH YOUR EMOTIONAL SELF

Last, but far from least, is your emotional self, which defies boundaries and tends to get louder during certain times of the month. Your emotional self is the realm of your feelings. It's where you experience joy, anger, sadness, excitement, fear, surprise, and disgust. Your emotions are an essential aspect of being human. They provide valuable information about what you're experiencing in any given moment. When you're in an open, healthy conversation with them, your emotions are a fabulous ally in life, alerting you to how you feel about a person or situation and guiding you to actions and behaviors that contribute to a balanced, fulfilling life. But when the conversation gets fuzzy and your emotional voice becomes muffled, it can be difficult to discern what your emotions are really asking for.

If you don't monitor them with a critical eye, your emotions can drive you to make decisions that feel really good in the moment but aren't good for you in the long run: eating the entire tub of mint chocolate chip ice cream, buying those shoes that cost way too much, or sending that angry text before reading it twice. Things like this happen every day because, fundamentally, we are emotional creatures. So much of how we move through the world is determined by how we are feeling, and mostly we don't want to feel bad. Feeling bad just doesn't feel good, and we'll do pretty much anything to avoid it. This is why concepts like "retail therapy" and "emotional eating" have so much power over us. If we don't make cheerleader tryouts or the person we've been crushing on all year is paying attention to someone else, we may try to soothe our tender hearts with a new shirt or an entire sleeve of Chips Ahoy! cookies.

I believe firmly in listening to *all* aspects of yourself, emotions very much included. Sometimes this listening means that you need to tend to yourself in a super-gentle, nurturing way, and, yes, this can look like binge watching *Girls* while eating Double Stuf Oreos in bed. But I want you to be such a warrior of balance, such a fierce ninja of health and wellness, that you will be able to discern when you really need baked goods and HBO and when you need to push yourself to move your body, reach out to a friend, or write in your journal. Emotions can be difficult to understand, but when you're dedicated to living a balanced life, you'll find that it's easier than ever to field the requests of your emotions without compromising the other aspects of yourself.

Becoming fluent in the languages of the other two aspects of yourself, your body and mind, is the best way to begin to respond to the language of your emotions, which are particularly tricky and manipulative if you don't stay one step ahead of them.

Remember, your body wants to be in balance. It wants to feel healthy, strong, and energized. If your body is communicating an imbalance through sluggishness, moodiness, bloating, or breakouts, you can bring your attention to the fuel you've been giving yourself and the exercise you've been getting and make necessary adjustments. As you become an increasingly skilled listener, you'll be able to tell when your body needs more or less of something. You'll know when you need a salad, if you didn't drink enough water today, or if it's time to work out. Can your emotional distress withstand good food and movement?

The same goes for your mind. When you're consumed with worry, stress, or anxiety, your mind is telling you that it can't function properly. To break the cycle and to find mental balance again, first notice your thoughts and then breathe. You may find that one negative idea is looping over and over again or that negative thoughts are piling on top of each other. By bringing attention to this, and then finding your breath, you release the pressure valve and reestablish calm and centeredness. Can uncomfortable feelings remain when you're in this new state of mind?

I want you to listen deeply and take a hard look at every message that you receive from each part of you. If you find yourself craving Cheetos and a Diet Coke, it's probably wise to engage in some inquiry before reaching for the orange bag. What's behind that longing for junk food? It's a safe bet that your body doesn't actually want those things—bodies want natural, whole foods and lots of water—so what part of you is really doing the asking? Some quick detective work may point you to your emotions. Ask yourself how you're feeling in the moment that the desire for Cheetos pops into your mind. Are you happy and

WHEN BAD IS GOOD

Human beings contain the whole universe of emotions, from agony and despair to happiness and bliss. Sure, it feels better to feel good, but the hard emotions are essential, too, and it's only by really feeling them that they will eventually go away. The next time you feel something challenging like disappointment or heartache, see if you can find the courage to actually settle into the emotion for a few minutes. This can be really scary at first. Our natural reaction to hard feelings is to look for a way out of feeling them. We do this by pushing them down with distractions like food, TV, or social media. But when we don't give tough feelings the opportunity to move through us, they stay embedded within us, which can lead to psychological or emotional challenges, or even illness, later in life. Dare yourself to feel your tough feelings. Pema Chödrön, a wise Buddhist nun and teacher, believes that it takes just 90 seconds for a hard feeling to vaporize. Bravely living with the feeling for only a minute and a half will lead you to relief!

COMPARISON SICKNESS

One of the quickest routes to feeling bad about yourself is to compare yourself to others. You know the feeling: You're cruising through the Instagram of the most popular girl in school, taking in her perfect bikini body, her cute boyfriend, and what looks like shots from a super-fun party, and a dark, murky sensation begins to move its way into your chest. You look down critically at your own body and think of your nonexistent boyfriend, and the murky feeling grows. Then you tell yourself that you are not smart enough, not pretty enough, not talented enough, not good enough. As the heavy sensation deepens in your chest, moving up to your throat, you actually start to feel unwell. I call this Comparison Sickness.

To find balance and live a fulfilling life, it's essential to click into the belief that you have something special to offer the world—because you do, even if you don't know it yet. There are so many inspirational people in the spotlight, sharing their gifts with us through performances (and Instagram), but nobody else is you. Honing your listening skills to hear the messages of your body, mind, and emotions will help you find what it is that inspires you, which will lead you to your purpose, your own journey. That's how it worked for me. My interest in dance led me to an interest in how the body works, which led me to helping people feel and look their best.

When you judge others from the outside, whether it's through stalking them on social media, watching them perform, or checking them out from across the cafeteria, you are mostly relying on your own invention, which has been pieced together from photo-shopped images and stolen glimpses. I often think about how I am presented to the world. Most people are familiar with me from my workout videos, from photo shoots I've done for magazines, or from books like this one! Each of those circumstances was staged. I was wearing hair extensions and tons of makeup applied by a professional makeup artist. The way I look on the screen or on the page is *not* how I look in everyday life. Instead of comparing yourself to others and making yourself sick, a much better use of your time would be to focus on yourself—spending time doing things that light you up, with people who make you feel good about who you are.

wanting to reward yourself a bit? Are you feeling bummed and wanting to soothe yourself in some way? Is a good friend or teammate digging into her own pack of cheesy snacks, and it feels good to share the experience? Each of these questions leads you right back to your emotions—you're either eating to reward, soothe, or connect.

This is where the emotions get tricky. They want you to think that your body is asking for junk food, but you're one step ahead. You've honed your listening skills, and you can hear who's actually doing the talking. You're now in a position to make a good decision for yourself. If you decide to eat the Cheetos and drink the Coke, you will do it because it is the right move for your emotional self. Hopefully, the decision will be made from a place of balance. You'll have to do a quick check-in to see if you've eaten relatively well during the week and if you'll be able to eat a healthy dinner that night. If so, a bag of Cheetos and a Coke probably won't be that harmful. But if you snack like this every day, it will begin to take a toll. This balance check-in can be done anytime you feel called upon to make a choice that may not be the healthiest.

Gratitude Bombing: Get Thankful!

We all go through phases where life just feels tough. Regardless of how hard you try, you just can't seem to get out of the rut. You may be having a difficult time with a friend, struggling in school or sports, or navigating a bumpy situation at home—or all of them at once. These are the times when it's really easy to feel that things are hopeless.

I've been there. There have been many times when I felt that life was not on my side, as if some unseen force was conspiring against me. I still remember how painful it was to see my dream of becoming a professional dancer fade away with every pound that I was unable to shed. And there was that period when my marriage to my son's father was ending and that time when I wasn't sure what direction my career was going to take.

Each of these moments was legitimately challenging, just like whatever you're going through is legitimately challenging, but I learned that things got harder when I continued to feel angry, resentful, or sorry for myself. These are all legitimate emotions, but if I stayed trapped in any of them for too long, I felt stuck and even more unhappy. It's important to allow whatever feelings you're having to surface; pushing them down is never a good idea. But when you're ready to start feeling good again, the quickest route to relief is gratitude.

It's really simple. Spend a few moments feeling thankful for the aspects of your life that are working. I call this Gratitude Bombing! There's always

CYCLE SAVVY

Everybody has moods that shift and change, but girls and women are especially prone to erratic feelings, especially during a certain time of the month. Understanding, and respecting, your menstrual cycle will help you navigate your changing moods and will guide you in making choices that will give you support when you need it most. I am a big believer in making an effort to tune in to where you are in your cycle throughout the month. Most girls have about a 28-day cycle (give or take a few days), and your hormones are busy doing different things throughout that window of time. As you pay attention to how you feel throughout the different stages of your cycle, you will be able to give yourself the care and attention that will make your experience easier, such as certain foods or more rest.

FIVE THINGS TO PRACTICE

CONNECT

1 START LISTENING
Recognize that in every moment, there are three parts of yourself vying for your attention: the physical, mental, and emotional. Becoming familiar with their individual languages, and wisely fielding their requests, will set you up to live a truly balanced life.

2 RECOGNIZE YOUR BODY'S MESSAGES
Your physical self requires fuel in the form of whole foods and water, as well as adequate rest. Ignore these needs and your system starts to break down. You may find that you're sluggish, bloated, overweight, or struggling with breakouts. Change your diet and note how your symptoms react.

3 TUNE IN TO YOUR MIND
A balanced mind is calm, alert, and peaceful. If you're feeling anxious, stressed, or overwhelmed, it's time to pay attention to your mental state. Tune in to the contents of your thoughts and notice their patterns. Are they looping or stacking? If so, breathe consciously until you find stable ground again.

4 FEED YOUR EMOTIONS (WITH AWARENESS)
Your emotional self has needs, too. Become aware of this tricky aspect of yourself by recognizing a true emotional need and giving in to it when appropriate. Sometimes you do require cookies and Netflix. But, more often, you need movement and support in the form of friends, family, or journaling.

5 GET GRATEFUL. STOP COMPARING
When in doubt, drop a Gratitude Bomb (or 20). Turning your attention to the things that are working in your life (there is *always* something that's working) will shift your energy to goodness. Before you know it, you'll be feeling better overall. And don't get Comparison Sickness. Use willpower and self-care to resist the urge to stalk celebrities or acquaintances on social media and to put anybody on a pedestal. Everybody is on his or her own journey. Focus on your own path.

something that's working. It could be as simple as feeling gratitude for having a healthy body or a best friend, for parents who love you, for a house that's warm and cozy, or for having food to eat. Feeling gratitude for the things that are working in your life will fill you with a sense of goodness that will start to grow, and before you know it, you may find yourself feeling better overall. Keep a gratitude journal where you can jot down your daily Gratitude Bombs. Keep it simple: *chocolate, warm autumn days, snuggling with my cat, my favorite purple shirt, Facetiming with my grandma.* See how many things you can list without thinking too hard.

Listening deeply to your physical, mental, and emotional selves will set you up to find balance—that dreamy place where you're feeling energized, alert, peaceful, and capable of achieving anything you set your mind to. As you explore what it means to tune in to the messages of the three parts of you, be patient and kind with yourself. Learning a new language takes time, and you're learning three! There will be days when you feel super-connected to one part of yourself; maybe it's your body that will be optimized, carrying you swiftly down the sports field or through your daily workout. You'll feel strong and agile. Or your mind may be working at its best, and you'll be feeling calm and clear, dazzling teachers and your fellow students with your sharp intellect and original ideas. Or it could be your emotional self that is shining. You're feeling grateful for all the good things that are in your life and peaceful and relaxed in your heart. With practice, you'll have moments when all three parts of yourself are operating at their best! This will likely be when you've been effectively listening to their individual needs and making choices that are best for your long-term health and happiness.

EAT

Adult women are the reason why I'm writing this book for teenagers. I've spent so much time working with ladies in their twenties, thirties, and beyond—I also happen to be one of those ladies—that I've become super-familiar with the things that help or hinder health and wellness goals. We tackled a big one in CONNECT, a lack of genuine self-love and appreciation for the real you, and here, in EAT, we'll look at another obstacle: unraveling a lifetime of toxic taste habits. As teens, you are in an incredible position to cut these harmful habits off before they get a serious hold on you, which will save you a lot of extra work and struggle later in life.

Once a woman becomes clear that she wants to live a healthier life and feel better in her body, she is required to take a very real look at how she eats (and how she moves, but you'll read about that in MOVE, starting on page 43). Unless you're being raised by professional nutritionists, this often means staring down an intimidating list of deeply ingrained toxic taste habits. There are a million ways to go wrong, from starting each day with a jelly doughnut and a diet soda, to eating only frozen prepared foods, to using refined carbohydrates like pasta and bread as the basis for most meals, to soothing hard emotions with processed snacks like Doritos or Oreos, to rarely eating leafy green veggies, to regularly eating fast food, to never drinking water, and the list goes on.

The longer we do something, the harder it is to stop doing it. This absolutely applies to eating and is the reason that I am so determined to help teenagers establish healthy food habits while they have tons of time on their side. If a 30-year-old woman has started her day with a doughnut and Diet Coke for the last 15 years, it is going to be incredibly challenging for her to greet the day with a wholesome breakfast that supports the needs of her body and mind. Not only does she have to push past the natural resistance that we all experience when faced with a different way of doing things—we're creatures of habit, and we get comfortable with the status quo—but she also has to let go of the emotional connection she's unknowingly attached to that doughnut and soda.

She's been starting the day with a sweet baked good for so many years because it stimulates her tastebuds (mmm . . . sugar, fat, refined carbohydrates) and also because it lights up memory centers in her brain that trigger an emotional reaction in her heart. That doughnut may remind her of the Pop-Tarts she ate every day during her middle school years or the dozen Dunkin' Donuts her grandpa bought her when she visited during school vacations or the chocolate chip muffins she shared with her high school field hockey team before away games. Every doughy, sugary bite unconsciously jolts her back to the comfort of childhood, where she felt safe and protected. The feeling is warm and fuzzy, but, wow, that's a ton of emotional weight for a simple doughnut to carry, and it's a guaranteed lose-lose deal for her body.

The doughnut causes her blood sugar to spike, leading to an inevitable mid-morning crash at the office. She finds that she can barely keep her head off the conference table at the 10:00 a.m. meeting, which causes her to drag herself to the nearest Starbucks at 11:00 a.m. for a Frappuccino (loaded with sugar and caffeine), starting the spike-crash-spike cycle all over again. Greeting the morning with her usual breakfast isn't great for productivity at work—her boss is starting to notice—and it's also derailing her wellness goals. She's been trying to lose 10 pounds for more than a year now, but she is emotionally addicted to these tastes and so maintains the toxic habit that began when she was a teen.

Meanwhile, the components of a simple, tasty power breakfast languish in her kitchen—eggs, spinach, avocado, and a handful of grated cheese, plus a mug of green tea to go with it. This nutrient-dense combination of protein, healthy fats, vitamins A and C, and powerful antioxidants would deliver sustainable energy that would keep her body and mind functioning at top level until lunchtime. But first she has to convince her tastebuds, and her heart, that it's safe to try something new. If you start today, while you are still young, you won't have to worry about untangling the knots of unhealthy eating habits when you are an adult—and your teenage self will thank you, too.

CARING FOR YOUR PHYSICAL SELF

We've explored the idea that the human body is like a vehicle that requires the right fuel and maintenance to run efficiently or a home that needs to be cleaned and maintained in order to provide comfort and safety for its inhabitants. I also believe that the body is like a computer that will perform well only if its operating system is optimized. Think about how your computer (or smartphone or tablet) gets glitchy or malfunctions if it has a virus or limited storage, or if you forget to update an app. The same goes for your body. If you're eating poor-quality food all day, every day, it becomes really difficult for your operating system to function at peak performance. Your computer will lose documents or freeze up if you don't maintain it. If you are consistently neglecting your body, it will also alert you that something is out of balance. You may find that you're struggling with acne, weight gain, dry hair, dull eyes, brittle nails, a fuzzy brain, moodiness, fatigue, lack of confidence, or even a weakened immune system. You may not realize that these symptoms are directly associated with the things you are putting in and on your body, as well as the way you are or aren't moving. But it is extremely important to listen to how your body feels and to look at how it functions.

Your body is designed to run on foods in their most natural state. I realize that it can be very challenging to find and keep fresh organic produce around at all times, or even to supply yourself with the cleanest protein options. You're probably restricted in your choices by a number of things—from time commitments, to school and extracurricular activities that make it hard for you to grocery shop or cook, to limited family support that might make buying organic, clean foods challenging. It is important that each of us learns to make our healthiest choices within the realities of each of our lives, so do your best, but compromise if needed. Maybe you can offer to cook the whole family dinner if your parents buy the groceries, or do the chopping and prep work if your mom or dad would rather do the cooking—find what works for you and your family.

While you are growing physically and shifting hormonally, you're learning at a forced rate. Coaches, teachers, and parents are pushing you to hit benchmark after benchmark, which can be exhausting! Your energy supplies can lag far behind your needs and lead to the suboptimal physical symptoms I described above. So take a breath and slow yourself down—you can do some things on your own time.

The changes and incredible benefits to your body that you will start to see once you make better food choices will also set the stage for you to focus more on the things that you want to achieve. You won't be as bothered by the stress that comes with feeling unhealthy and out of sync with your body. You will not be distracted by food trends and suckered by false marketing campaigns, because you will feel knowledgeable about food and in control of your choices. You will be able to discern what is good advice and what is bad, and you won't be swayed when others defend their extreme diets and try to convince you to try them.

First and foremost, you have to learn to listen to your body, and not just its impulses. When a craving emerges, when you see a pizza or a bag of cookies and are tempted to dig in, you need to learn to let every part of you into the conversation. Your emotional urge can't be the only thing speaking. Take a simple breath and check in with your intellectual self; ask it whether it can come up with a better option than the cookies or pizza, one that might still make your emotional self happy. Then ask your physical self whether your body needs cookies. Perhaps your physical self knows that eating unhealthfully at 8:00 a.m., say, won't allow you to do your best throughout the day. Your intellectual self will surely support your physical intuition that cookies or pizza for breakfast is not the best choice. But still you need to recognize your emotional needs and find another meal that can allow you to walk away from temptation.

Now, if it's 8:00 a.m. and you're hungry and getting on a long bus ride for a field trip, and there is no good food in the house, it may be either the cookies, cold pizza, or nothing. Although it's not ideal, in this situation, the physical and intellectual selves would understand the necessity of eating something to fuel your body. But you need to learn how to have these conversations, and learn how to weigh and balance negative and positive food choices, because they matter. Don't eat mindlessly. Think through your decisions, even the ones that end in cookies.

If you aren't at an unhealthy weight, and you do eat vegetables most days, having leftover pizza for breakfast on one busy morning is going to be totally fine. However, even if you don't have any weight issues, I wouldn't recommend eating pizza every day. I would worry about general health issues and intolerances that could arise from such an unbalanced diet. My hope is that you'll be super-inspired to change the way you eat because you want a body that is as strong and healthy as possible and one that will age as smoothly as possible.

But let's first look at why many teens don't put a focus on healthy eating in the first place. There are lots of factors that contribute to teens eating poorly. To be fair, many teenagers don't have full control over the food options they are given—meals are often served by your family, or the cafeteria, or a friend's parent. The way you eat is also influenced by how much money you have to spend and how jam-packed your schedule is on any given day (it's called fast food for a reason). Yet I think teens lean toward junk food because doing so plays right into a universal part of the teenage years: the invincibility myth.

Teens tend to think they can do anything and survive. This superhero belief system is a necessary part of growing up. You need to be armed with the daydream that you can do anything in order to ignite the courage to try new things. But believing that you can do anything can also be a dangerous mindset, even when it comes to something as simple as eating. Millions of teenagers operate as if their youth creates a sort of supersonic force field that keeps them safe from the harmful effects of junk food. You may have recently tested this theory by indulging in a Reese's Peanut Butter Cup eating contest or eating a Big Mac 7 days in a row.

You ate the junk food, you may or may not have felt queasy afterward, and you lived. That's evidence enough that it's okay to eat like this, right? Wrong. Most teens think that they can get away with poor food choices because they don't see the immediate consequences of their actions. If you eat french fries and ice cream all day long, you'll still wake up every day, go to school, practice soccer, fight with your sister, empty the dishwasher, and so on. But I'm here to tell you that what you eat today sets the stage for how you feed yourself later in life (think of that 30-year-old and her doughnut breakfast) and how healthy you remain as you age.

Your teenage body may have the defenses necessary to combat the unhealthy choices you make today—Big Macs, excessive tanning, sleep deprivation, cookie binges—but your 30-year-old or 50-year-old body may have a tougher time remaining in balance. Your body chemistry changes as you age; a young body has an ability to combat harmful influences and regenerate and recover that fades as you get older. If you create healthy habits when you are young, you will be able to carry them into every stage of your life. But it's important to remember that eating right doesn't only prepare you for a vibrant adulthood; it impacts your life, right here, right now. Change the way you eat, and you'll feel the effects almost immediately. You'll have more energy, fewer mood swings, and brighter skin and hair. Stick with a healthy eating plan, and you'll feel stronger, happier, and more beautiful overall.

I get that eating in a new way can be intimidating at any age. I see it all the time in my adult clients who ask me, with fear in their eyes, if they have to give up their daily chocolate chip scone or their grandma's lasagna. They ask because food does so much more than keep us alive. It's comfort, joy, celebration, connection, and a daily lifeline that we turn to three times a day (plus snacks). Perhaps you're thinking, *I'm nice and comfy with the foods that are currently in my repertoire, thank you very much.* Maybe you've been starting the morning with an Eggo waffle slathered with butter and syrup and a tall chocolate milk every day since you were 6. Maybe pizza has been, and will always be, your comfort food of choice. I totally understand. It would be a brave soul who tries to take away my ice cream or dark chocolate treats, but I keep them close to me because they are a small part of a bigger diet based entirely on whole foods.

HOW DID THAT FOOD MAKE ME FEEL?

As you strive to change the way you eat so you can improve the way you look, feel, and show up in the world, it's important to pay close attention to how foods affect you directly after you eat them. Start right where you are. Eat your usual breakfast and note how it makes you feel. A journal is a great tool here. Date each page and quickly jot down what you consumed and how it made you feel after 15 minutes, 1 hour, and 3 hours. Pay attention to your energy levels (are you alert? sluggish? jittery?), your mental clarity (is your mind foggy, or are you thinking clearly?), and the state of your stomach (is it calm? gurgling? heavy?).

If trying new foods and flavors feels risky, even unpleasant at first, I'm going to ask you to take the risk. It'll be worth it. The unhealthy eating patterns that are part of your current life as a teenager may lead to much more than excess weight and poor food choices when you're older. They can also directly influence your health in pretty scary ways. More adults than ever—and some teens, too—are living with type 2 diabetes, heart disease, and obesity, diseases that almost always stem from consistently choosing foods high in saturated fat, sugar, and salt.

I don't want you to give up every flavor or dish that makes you happy. I'm the first one to encourage my clients to indulge at the holiday meal or to go out to that very special restaurant on that very special date. Eating is a significant part of our social fabric, creating a path to connection and shared good times. The food we eat together is at the heart of so many beautiful memories. I want every teen and woman I work with to be able to enjoy food with friends and family. It's important that you participate in the team celebration or class party or share a cozy meal with friends. Your tastebuds are an essential part of who you are, and they should not be denied.

That said, I want you to be a smart and savvy guardian, poised firmly at the gates of your body. You are how you nourish; it's important to decide wisely what foods you let in. You are the gatekeeper.

Listening carefully to the three parts of yourself, you can make decisions that honor the needs of your body, mind, and emotions. Your emotional self may tell you that eating your grandfather's famous triple chocolate brownies will not only make your tastebuds jump for joy, but it will also make his heart swell with pride and happiness when he sees how happy they make you. Listen to the message you're receiving here, but take it in as part of a bigger picture. If you eat this dessert, your emotions will be content, but your body is likely going to need a rest from fat and sugar for a few days. Can you respect that message, too? That's the balance we're always seeking.

I ask my clients to approach eating from a place of purity and respect, and I give the same guidance to you. Instead of mindlessly reaching for whatever food is right there or whatever food everyone else is eating, I encourage you to remember that you are in charge. You are the one who controls what kind of fuel your body will run on for the rest of the day. Choosing whole foods whenever possible sets you up for success in all you do.

IS THIS REAL FOOD?

Most of us eat unconsciously until a friend or family member (or book!) wakes us up to what we're consuming each day. As you bring renewed attention to what you're putting into your body, there is one key question that will be your trusted guide along the way: *Is this real food?* As soon as you open your eyes each morning, I want you to prepare yourself to ask that question before putting a morsel of food into your mouth for the rest of the day.

But what is real food? Isn't all food real? Not even close. Real food is another name for "whole foods," and when it comes to eating what will help you live your best, most balanced life yet, whole foods are what it's all about. Whole foods are the surest path to a strong and vital body, at a weight that is optimal for your frame and lifestyle. A "whole" food is just that—a food that has not been altered in any way. It comes to you in its most pure, original form, and you eat it just as it is.

I love whole foods! I am absolutely dedicated to a whole foods diet and insist that anybody who is serious about improving their health and restoring balance to their body, mind, and emotions must commit to a diet that is composed almost completely of real foods, because they are nutritional powerhouses. Whole foods are nutrient dense, which means that they deliver essential nutrients that your body requires to run efficiently, such as fiber, vitamins, and minerals, with no added sugar or fat. Basically, your body loves whole foods.

On the other side, tempting us with the glow of a neon-orange cheesy coating, the crunch of the crispy, the sugar-coated, and the fried, is processed food. Processed foods are the polar opposite of whole foods. These foods are energy dense; they provide lots of calories but little to no nutritional value for your body. To answer the pressing question, *No, they are not real*. Cheez Doodles, Doritos, potato chips, Hot Pockets, Pop-Tarts, any kind of packaged baked goods, boxed mac and cheese, microwave popcorn, pretty much anything that comes out of a vending machine—these are all processed foods. Processed food is *made, not grown*. If you are questioning whether or not a food is processed, do a bit of investigating into its origins. A whole food is made of one ingredient: itself. A processed food consists of several ingredients, usually with added sugar, salt, and fat to make it taste better.

There was a time when whole foods were all that people consumed. Food was grown on farms, not created in a factory. Meals were comprised primarily of vegetables, fruits, meats, and grains, i.e., foods that needed to be cultivated and harvested before you could eat them. This was all fine and good until people began looking for ways to eat faster and cheaper. Around the beginning of the 20th century, moms longed for a way to feed their families with less effort, and the military needed a less expensive way to feed the troops. Enter the era of processed foods. Some of the first mass-produced foods to hit the market are still some of our country's favorites: Nathan's hot dogs, Oreo cookies, Marshmallow Fluff, Welch's grape jelly, Velveeta cheese, Kraft Macaroni & Cheese. These foods are made in bulk by machines in a factory, using inexpensive ingredients, and then they are shipped all over the country. Strong chemical preservatives guarantee that they can collect dust on any supermarket or gas station shelf for years without going bad.

The long-lasting popularity of some of the biggest names in processed foods (Kraft Mac & Cheese was introduced to the public in 1937!) shows you that it's clearly more than the price point and ease-of-use that make these products appealing. These foods taste good! Seriously good. So good, in fact, that the companies that make them caught on quickly to the money-making potential of their products, spending billions in research and development to create products that were even more irresistible. I see these as the super-villains of the

SPOT THE WHOLE FOODS

Take a trip to your kitchen and see how many processed foods you can find. Potato? Whole food. Instant mashed potatoes? Processed food. Banana? Whole food. Box of store-bought banana nut muffins? Processed food. Ear of corn? Whole food. Corn chips? Processed food. Think you've got it? Keep going! Pork chop? Whole food. Hot dog? Processed food. How many can you find?

YOU CAN'T HEAR IF IT ISN'T QUIET

The body is equipped with smart devices that alert you when there is a deficiency taking place; it will tell you what it needs through your cravings. You may need iron if you're craving red meat, or vitamin C if you're longing for citrus fruit. These messages can be quite subtle. To tune in to what your physical self is saying, you have to be able to hear it. You turn down the noise by breaking your junk food habit. If food was assigned a volume, processed food would be on level 10. Its manufactured flavors are bold and brassy and block out the soft messages that your body may be trying to communicate. When junk food is an everyday part of your life, you get stuck in a cycle of indulgence and can completely lose the ability to hear your body's true needs.

junk food universe. There are too many to name, but they stretch from Betty Crocker Brownie Mix, Ragú Tomato Sauce, Cool Ranch Doritos, Hot Pockets, Cap'n Crunch cereal, lunchmeat, and beyond. Each of these foods was specifically designed to light up our tastebuds in ways that we're almost powerless against. Almost.

Most of the processed food you eat was engineered in a lab by scientists who get paid to decode how your tastebuds, brain, and stomach function. They figured out that there is a trifecta of ingredients that makes our mouths deliriously happy: sugar, salt, and fat. The right combination of these three will make a food dance across your tongue and stimulate the same pleasure points in your brain that a drug addict experiences when he shoots up heroin or snorts cocaine. *Did I just compare Cool Ranch Doritos to cocaine? Yes.* You can't overdose on Doritos or damage every aspect of your life with the habit, but indulge often enough, and you are creating a standard of eating that will have long-term negative effects on your health and your waistline.

We're onto what junk food companies are doing thanks to folks like author Michael Moss. This intrepid *New York Times* reporter—and father—revealed the science behind our junk food addiction in his bestselling book, *Salt Sugar Fat: How the Food Giants Hooked Us.* He spent 3 years investigating the food industry and discovered firsthand how those three ingredients pull us down into a rabbit hole of insatiable cravings. Salt creates a burst of flavor that satisfies us deeply, and it also masks the unpleasant flavor of the high-powered preservatives that manufacturers use to give foods that epic shelf life. Sugar is a flavor that human beings crave naturally from birth (breast milk is sweet), and food developers exploit that desire ruthlessly by adding sugar to products way beyond desserts. It doesn't take much label sleuthing to see that sugar is tucked into bread, yogurt, even tomato sauce. Savvy food scientists also understand that our brains will tell our stomachs that we've had enough if something is too sweet, so sugar is kept at a magical "bliss point," where you crave more without feeling full too fast. And fat is the final magical ingredient. Foods that boast lots of fat provide us with a deeply satisfying experience called mouth feel;

think of the jolt of pleasure you experience when you eat that first spoonful of cookie dough ice cream or sink your teeth into a melty grilled cheese. That delightful, silky smooth sensation that coats the tongue and makes us indescribably happy is courtesy of fat.

The manipulative powers of processed foods don't end there. The brilliant minds behind snacks like cheese puffs figured out that the puffs would be endlessly enticing if they landed on your tongue in a pouf of cheesy, salty, fatty goodness and then melted away before your teeth even had a chance to get involved in the situation. It's called vanishing caloric density, and it means that your brain doesn't have time to register the food, or its calories, before it disappears forever—so you automatically reach for another one to re-create the experience. And another. And another.

When you look closely at what the big food companies are doing, it's easy to feel frustrated and angry; they are making money at the expense of our health, and teaching our palates that food tastes good only if it's drowning in sugar, salt, and fat. This is why you may have a hard time eating whole foods at first. The clean, simple sweetness of a carrot (full of vitamins A and C plus fiber) has a hard time competing with the sugary pop of a processed carrot muffin loaded with refined sugar, saturated fat, and white flour. Same goes for a crisp, sweet apple (big on vitamin C, potassium, and fiber) versus a store-bought apple pie, also jammed with refined sugar and saturated fat.

There's no way around it: Our bodies are designed to eat whole foods. The body recognizes that real foods bring vital nutrients to us—they are life giving! You can get all of your required nutrition from a balanced whole foods diet: vegetables, fruits, lean proteins, and some grains. When you eat like this, you are giving yourself the best fuel possible and preparing yourself to be the best *you* possible. Your brain will work at an optimal level, your body will feel strong and capable, and you will look healthy and vibrant, with your skin glowing, hair shiny, and eyes bright and clear. When you eat a whole foods diet, you won't

IT'S NOT ALL BAD NEWS

As we become increasingly aware of what's actually in processed foods and continue to make the connection between what we eat and the health epidemics that are raging through this country, the processed food giants are beginning to listen and make changes. Some are starting to reformulate their most popular food items, taking huge amounts of salt out of the middle of their recipes and putting less on top, reformulating fat globules so they're thinner and broader and less damaging to the body, and decreasing the sugar content of items that really don't require sugar to taste good. While this is good news, and shows that big food manufacturers are finally paying attention to what the public is consuming, it doesn't change the fact that the body wants whole foods. If you must indulge in a processed food, take the time to check out what's really in it, but whenever possible, choose foods that haven't been made in a factory.

need to pile on the makeup or use masking filters on Instagram—you will be in balance and naturally beautiful.

Eating in balance, for balance, involves a bit of a learning curve at first—an *unlearning* curve, really. Eating processed food is addicting. Junk food quickly hits the reward centers in the brain, which feels really good in the moment. And because these foods are low in fiber and high in sugar (which means they are digested quickly), they give you a quick jolt of energy that inevitably leads to a crash. This is why you may turn to more junk food later in the day, seeking out another energy boost, often in the form of caffeine and more sugar—*hello, Starbucks.* The journey to sustainable, longer-lasting energy, and a body in balance, starts with unlearning what tastes good and creating new flavor relationships. If your only idea of a good time is a 100-person party with fireworks and DJs, it's going to be tough for you to enjoy yourself at a dinner with one or two friends. Same goes for eating. If your yummy light is lit only by processed foods like Ding Dongs and french fries, it may be a stretch, at first, to find satisfaction from the subtler flavors of a salad or a piece of fruit. Your palate has to adjust to these new tastes, and it will, as it quickly notes how your body responds to nutrient-dense whole foods.

The foods you eat also build on each other. If you wake up in the morning to a bowl of Honey Nut Cheerios and milk, you may enjoy the taste and receive a little energy, but you will crash an hour and a half into school. But if you start your day with a hard-cooked egg and a bowl of berries, you give your body cleaner, longer-lasting energy. And when you get hungry again, you'll find that you're craving a whole foods snack of almonds or of whole grain crackers and peanut butter instead of gummy bears or Chips Ahoy! cookies.

GO ORGANIC

I love the idea of helping young women take steps to find balance in their bodies, minds, and hearts so they can pursue their dreams. The shift to a primarily whole foods diet is an absolutely essential aspect of this balance—there's no way around it. All day, every day, you must ask the question, *Is this real food?* and then make eating choices that support or block your journey to balance and vitality. When considering what to eat, it's also useful to look into whether a food is organic. Organic foods are grown without the use of synthetic pesticides, herbicides, or hormones. These chemicals are difficult for the body to process and can lead to health challenges down the road.

Again, I understand that you might not always have full control over your food options when you're sitting at your parents' dining room table or in your school cafeteria. But there will be opportunities for you to choose between an organic option or a conventional (nonorganic) option, or, even better, you may be able to influence or inspire your family or school to bring more organic foods to the table. Growing fruits or vegetables with chemicals and raising animals that are given additional hormones allows factory farms to produce more of those foods for less money. This means that organic options are more expensive, but there are ways to get more organic bang for your buck. All it takes is a bit of food know-how, which means understanding what conventional foods are the worst offenders and seeking out organic alternatives whenever possible.

When it comes to produce, the Environmental Working Group's Dirty Dozen is an excellent shopping and eating guide (see "The Dirty Dozen" at right). Visit the EWG's website (ewg.org) for additional support for all aspects of clean living, including up-to-date reports on conventional foods to avoid as well as suggestions for personal care products that are safe to use (did you know that your deodorant or shampoo may contain harmful synthetic ingredients?). Beyond produce, it's also important to choose organic dairy products whenever possible. Organic milk, cheese, and yogurt are made with milk from cows that didn't receive any antibiotics or hormones and consumed a diet of 100 percent organic feed. That's good news for your body.

Part of becoming a fierce gatekeeper for anything that you take into your body is becoming knowledgeable about the origins of every bite of food that lands on your fork, whether it's produce, dairy, or animal protein. You've got your Dirty Dozen list (take a picture so it's in your phone for reference), and you now know that organic dairy is always best. But it can feel a bit overwhelming as you and your family try to understand what's happening with meat and eggs. There's *organic, grass fed, free range, cage free,* and so on. What's best?

THE DIRTY DOZEN

Some foods are worse chemical offenders than others. If you do nothing else, try to avoid consuming the conventional versions of the following 12 foods, which the Environmental Working Group (EWG) has determined are the most contaminated. If you're tempted to bite into that nonorganic strawberry, keep in mind that scientists at the USDA found that strawberries contained an average of 7.7 different pesticides per sample (compared to 2.3 pesticides per sample for all other produce).

Strawberries	Cherries
Spinach	Grapes
Nectarines	Celery
Apples	Tomatoes
Peaches	Sweet bell peppers
Pears	Potatoes

Here's a quick cheat sheet:

♥ Organic meat is raised free from chemical pesticides, chemical fertilizers, antibiotics, hormones, and genetically modified organisms (GMOs).

♥ Grass-fed beef means that the cattle were allowed to forage for their own food instead of subsisting on a diet of grains. This is a plus as grass is high in nutrients like omega-3s and B vitamins, leading to meat that is leaner and, some even say, more flavorful.

♥ Organic chicken is similar. The birds are fed organic feed (free from animal by-products, antibiotics, and genetically engineered grains and grown without synthetic pesticides or fertilizers) and are raised without the use of antibiotics or hormones and are given outdoor access to roam freely.

♥ Free-range birds are given outdoor access as well. When chickens are raised in crowded coops, they can become anxious, and those stress hormones are held in the bird's muscle tissue and then end up on your dinner plate.

♥ If you have an influence on the eggs that are purchased at home, look for "organic" eggs. The hens behind those eggs are fed organic feed, are cage-free, and are given outdoor access, though the amount of space they roam may be quite limited.

♥ Even better, look for "pasture-raised" eggs. Pasture-raised eggs come from chickens that have an even better life. They are moved to a different patch of land every day and given a chance to eat grasses and insects as well as their organic feed. Research is finding that eggs from pasture-raised hens may be healthier, too, with $2\frac{1}{2}$ times more omega-3s and twice the vitamin E of caged eggs from hens raised in cages and fed conventional mash.

The kind of seafood you eat is important as well. Fish is an excellent source of protein, and fish such as salmon, mackerel, and sardines are high in essential omega-3 fatty acids. But before you hit up your local fishmonger, keep in mind that most fish are factory farmed. These fish are raised in packed environments, which cause them to become stressed, which in turn compromises their immune systems, leading to illness, parasitic infections, and disease. To manage all this sickness, the fish are given lots of drugs, including antibiotics, and booster shots of sex hormones to encourage procreation, all of which ends up on your fork. Purchasing wild-caught fish allows you to avoid these contaminants.

UNDERSTANDING YOUR CYCLE, YOUR CRAVINGS, AND HOW TO FEED YOURSELF IN DIFFERENT SITUATIONS

Part of eating in balance is understanding that you're not going to eat the same way throughout the month. It's not a coincidence that you always crave chocolate and croissants 3 days before your period. Your cravings are signals that your body sends out when it needs more of something. In the case of chocolate and French pastries, it's telling you that it needs more calories to support the energetic output of menstruation. Instead of forcefully ignoring these very specific cravings, or indulging them unconsciously, I want you to use your trained ear to hear your body's call and discern a genuine craving from emotional trickery. Your body's hormone levels shift throughout the month, taking your energy levels and nutritional needs with them. Being prepared for these changes allows you to cater to cravings without allowing them to dominate your diet. The key is to acknowledge and address the craving without carrying it into the next phase of the month. This requires even more listening and data gathering.

Start paying attention to your cycles. Note what you feel like physically throughout the month. You'll start to see a pattern and likely notice that each of the 4 weeks is quite different. Do your breasts get tender a week before your period or during menstruation? Do you get cramps? Are you extra tired in the days leading up to your period? You'll also want to tune in emotionally: When are you extra happy? When are you sensitive or sad? Also bring awareness to your food cravings at each stage of the month. Are there days when you crave sweet foods or salty foods, carbs or chocolate? Pay attention to your subtle longing for french fries, Oreos, or bread and butter. Do the cravings fade after your period has arrived or after it is over?

You can keep a journal to track these fluctuations and variations, or you can use an awesome tracking app like Clue (available at the app store and at helloclue.com) to keep track of your cycles. Tracking will help you prepare for mood swings, cravings, and fatigue, allowing you to give yourself what you truly need throughout the month. This could be croissants, extra sleep, or the simple understanding that you're going to be grumpy for a few days (it helps to share this information with your friends and family).

Paying attention to your cycle is part of a bigger picture: paying attention to where you are in every given moment. Your goal is to do the best that you can throughout each day to nourish yourself with the most nutrient-dense foods available. You are now armed with the knowledge that processed foods lead to fatigue and brain fog. That soda and blueberry muffin may taste good going down, but it won't hold you through a rigorous calculus test and a late afternoon soccer game against your biggest rival. Made primarily of sugar and refined white flour, those choices will not give you sustainable energy. A better breakfast would be steel-cut oats with a tablespoon of organic almond butter with walnuts and blueberries and a splash of almond milk. The whole grain oats take longer to digest than a baked good made with refined white flour, giving you longer-lasting energy. The almond butter and walnuts provide necessary protein (great for brain power), and the blueberries provide fiber and powerful antioxidants (nutrients that help to prevent disease).

I understand that a hot whole foods breakfast may not be an option if you're running out the door. In that case, you could quickly spread some organic almond or peanut butter on whole grain toast with some sliced apple or banana. Boom! Power breakfast on the go. Wherever you are—whether it's your family's kitchen table, the school cafeteria, your best friend's house, out to dinner with your grandparents, on the bus on the way to an away game, at rehearsal for the play you're in— scan the environment for the foods that will be the cleanest, purest form of energy.

Preparation helps. If you know that you're going to be traveling to an away game where the only snack options will be junk food from the vending machines, fortify yourself with some better food options. Or if you're going to be at rehearsal into dinnertime and the cast usually orders in from a local fast-food joint, come armed with food that feeds you better. You can throw a snack pack of almonds, a bag of organic tortilla chips, a chicken sandwich, or a hard-cooked egg and an apple into your backpack. If the team makes a pit stop at a Burger King on the way home, know that it's okay to feed yourself food that fuels you right. While your teammates are digging into french fries and cheeseburgers, packed with salt and saturated fat, you'll have a whole food option that will carry you all the way to dinner or to breakfast the next morning.

That said, sometimes you won't be prepared. Clients ask me all the time if it's better to skip eating

Never skip eating entirely. Your body is counting on you to feed it. Instead ask: *What can I feed my body right now that will be a bridge until I get to some better food options?*

if there are no whole food options available. My answer is always the same: You are in a relationship with your body, and relationships are built on trust. When your body is legitimately hungry, you need to feed it; it's counting on you to do so. Imagine this: You just wrapped a big soccer game or volleyball tournament (enter your sport of choice here), and you're starving—your body needs to refuel. There are no whole foods to be seen; it's a sea of pizza, potato chips, and soda, and you forgot to pack some backup options. Even with these poor food options, muscling through your hunger is not the best choice. Your body worked hard for you and wants to be fed. When you ignore what it's saying, you are telling it that you are not listening; you are using too much willpower. Instead, I want you to give yourself the best food, working with what's available. In this scenario, one slice of pizza and some water from the water fountain could do it. If you are at McDonald's, it would be the smallest thing you can order to give yourself some necessary sustenance in the moment; a fish sandwich or Happy Meal could work. The question here is: *What can I feed my body right now that will serve as a bridge until I get to some better food options?*

You should also consider every aspect of your lifestyle when you're choosing what to eat. When available, whole foods are always the way to go, but it's also important to factor in what kind of energy you burn each day and the appropriate fuel you need to keep yourself humming along at an optimal level. Somebody who is a high scholastic achiever is going to need a different kind of fuel than someone who is more focused on athletic pursuits. This requires additional data gathering; to remain in balance, you must take a personal calculation about where you stand in every moment—bigger picture and close up. Bigger picture: Is it field hockey season, requiring you to be in top physical form on the field 6 days a week? Or is this your off-season for sports, and you're spending more time practicing a musical instrument or mastering a class that's particularly challenging? Close up: Are you right in the middle of your PMS week? Did you sleep poorly for the past few nights (we crave salty and fatty foods when we are fatigued)? Are you feeling down about something in your personal life? The answers to these questions will influence what you eat and how often you do so.

CELEBRATE WISELY

As we explored in CONNECT, your emotional self needs to be fed, too, and this is often done by rewarding yourself with a treat, soothing yourself with a treasured comfort food, or allowing yourself to share in a celebration with your friends, family, or community. When you prioritize clean eating, choosing veggies, fruits, lean proteins, and whole grains *most* of the time, you give yourself room to have fun with food some of the time. My entire career is based on healthful living (leafy green veggies are practically overflowing out of my fridge), yet I won't deny myself the occasional thoughtful indulgence, like my grandma's homemade chicken and noodles with mashed potatoes and gravy (serious yum!). You may have a soft spot for apple pie with vanilla ice cream or your favorite pasta dish. You get to decide what's right for your body, mind, and emotions.

This is especially true during the endless celebrations that happen during the holidays. Food is often at the center of every party, whether it's a birthday, Christmas dinner, or a pre-vacation shindig at school. Before you dive into the buffet or force yourself to nibble on nothing but a carrot, I encourage you to assess the situation: Who's throwing the party? What is the occasion? How important is the food to the host? You strike balance in celebratory situations by asking yourself if it feels wrong to refrain from sharing in the dining experience that's being offered. These assessments will be on a case-by-case basis, requiring you to consider the feelings of those who have planned the party or are participating in it, while simultaneously being an advocate for your own health. If you're taking a German class and your teacher has brought in a homemade Black Forest cake (a national treat of Germany), eating a piece is probably the right thing to do. If the party is meaningful to a friend, family member, coach, or teacher, participating would be kind. However you choose to join in, by filling your plate, or taking just a taste, never forget that you are always in control. You can participate in the celebration in your unique way. Only you know what your body and emotions are asking for; standing strong for what you need will fill you with strength and beauty.

The same rules of inquiry apply when using food to smooth the rough edges of a hard day or to bring tenderness to a hurting heart. You must use

> When you prioritize clean, whole foods, choosing veggies, fruits, lean proteins, and whole grains most of the time, you give yourself room to have fun with food some of the time.

EAT FIVE THINGS TO PRACTICE

1 MAKE THE SWITCH TO WHOLE FOODS
Start trading processed foods for whole foods. They are nutritionally dense and most easily assimilated by your body. Lean on my recipes for easy, tasty meals and on-the-go snacks.

2 GET CYCLE SAVVY
Use a cycle-tracking app to record how you feel at every stage of your monthly cycle. This will help you give yourself appropriate self-care, including foods that will serve you best physically and emotionally.

3 KEEP A FOOD JOURNAL
Pay attention to how different foods make you feel and what cravings you have during different stages of your cycle. This will help you to hone your listening skills so you can give your body the foods that it needs.

4 BE PREPARED
Don't get caught without a whole food option. Pack and take healthy snacks and lunches with you to beat back the after-school munchies and keep you fortified after away games.

5 CELEBRATE WISELY
Occasionally indulging in your favorite foods is important, especially when you're at a celebration with friends or family. Learn how to enjoy these flavors without getting stuck in a cycle of unhealthy eating.

Extra credit: Read *Salt Sugar Fat* by Michael Moss and watch *Fast Food Nation* (available on Amazon).

your listening skills to ascertain the appropriate action. If some ice cream and a Netflix binge will help you feel better, don't keep yourself from the gustatory healing. But even as you dig into the mocha chip, keep one antenna up. This will be the guidepost that will ensure that you don't cross over the fine line separating self-care from harming yourself with the indulgence—this could look like eating a bowlful versus eating the whole pint. Walking this line takes awareness and discernment. I practice this all the time! If I have a really stressful day, I may give myself french fries or tortilla chips and guacamole or even a hot fudge sundae. I'll give myself one portion, enjoy it deeply, and then get back to my baseline of balanced living. You can do it, too!

Eating in balance means that you know how to delight in the joy and connection that food brings. I find that people fall into danger zones when they can't find balance and choose to live primarily in a state of deprivation. When someone is driven by the vanity of getting to a certain weight, they often pull themselves out of the celebratory aspects of food, depriving themselves of all that joy and goodness, and become emotionally numb in the process. Cutting yourself off entirely from community and fun is just as extreme as eating ice cream cake every night for dinner. You're going to fall out of balance either way. It also helps to keep in mind that your weight is going to fluctuate. Most women experience a 5- to 10-pound fluctuation in their weight, depending on the time of the month and what's going on in their lives. As teens, you are going to go through those monthly changes, plus the shifts that are a natural part of growing. Paying attention to all aspects of your life—on the inside and the outside—will guide you to making the best eating choices for yourself at all times.

MOVE

SECTION 3

Movement is a fundamental part of being a human being.

From the moment we're born, we wiggle, shake, contract, and release. In less than 2 years, human babies learn to roll over, sit, crawl, pull up to a standing position, and take those first tentative steps. At that point, it's on! We run, jump, climb, and dance. Moving is an essential piece of who we are, keeping us engaged, fit, and alive. But as we transition out of the safety of our parents' arms and begin exploring the world around us, we quickly realize that we can fall and, when we fall, we may get hurt. We make the connection between toppling over and bumping our heads, or slipping and scraping our knees. Later, when we move from the seclusion of our living rooms and backyards to neighborhood playgrounds, school gymnasiums, and sports fields, our self-consciousness starts to kick in. We question how we're moving, wondering if it's good enough, and ask ourselves: *Do I look funny when I run? Do I look silly when I dance? Am I showing up for my team?* This self-doubt builds throughout childhood, often blossoming during the teenage years and following us into adulthood. These limiting thoughts block our freedom of expression and, most tragically, prevent us from building and maintaining an open and enjoyable relationship with our bodies.

When I work with adult clients, this disconnection from the body is hugely apparent. So many women have forgotten how to be vibrantly connected to their physicality. They aren't happy in their bodies and have no sense of what it's like to feel strong and fit. After years of sitting in front of their computers and TVs and comparing themselves to others, they've basically abandoned their bodies, choosing instead to live in their heads. I meet so many women who hope to lose weight and feel healthy and attractive, but before they can do so, they must reignite their natural connection to movement.

Many of the adult women who come to me have been lost in self-doubt for decades, continually questioning how they look and how they move. They tell themselves things like, *I'm not coordinated enough to take that dance class; I don't have the skills to join the company softball team; I'm not flexible enough for yoga; I'll always be overweight*. They may even be truly trying to make a change, dieting, exercising, playing sports. Yet they continue to battle their weight and struggle to find weight management solutions. They search for explanations and wonder, *Why isn't all my hard work paying off? Am I doing it wrong? Is something wrong with my body or my willpower?*

Unfortunately, they start to look for something to blame for their "failure" to look a certain way. They cease to see themselves as individuals and instead put themselves in categories. They say, "I have my grandmother's hips" or "My mom holds her weight in her stomach and arms, and so do I." If they have had kids, they say, "I lost my shape when I had babies." Women need a reason, but really the reason is that they have lost their physical connection with themselves at the deepest level.

We women are fed countless "get slim quick" scams. Often, we try them! Nearly every diet is set up for an immediate 10-pound weight loss, but most are almost impossible to sustain. When we gain weight back, we blame ourselves and not the diet, which did make us thinner at first. We are human beings; we must eat to live, but we also eat to celebrate, to emote, and to heal nutrient imbalances. Many times we aren't assuaging our physical hunger, but turning to food for other reasons. Extreme dieting doesn't just take away our food, it also keeps us from staying in touch with other important parts of who we are.

I believe that we must learn to eat for every reason that we need food, for every part of us—all of the three selves: physical and mental and emotional. You can always make smart, healthy choices without depriving yourself of good foods. Our overall well-being always comes first. For the most part, we can't just diet, diet, diet. We can't live with food restrictions, or we will begin to dream about food and shame ourselves for wanting things that we can safely consume and may even need for nourishment, both physical and emotional.

When I am meeting with a client who truly needs to lose weight, the most important first step is movement. Moving is absolutely vital to successful weight management. Often, someone will try to delay this step and say, "As soon as I diet off these extra 20 pounds, I'll start moving again and take a class." This is the wrong approach! They will need time to learn to commit to the dieting part of their journey back to health; they will need time to learn to commit to moving again, and to master their exercise routine. Once they no longer have such sedentary habits, and they have improved upon their physical performance, a piece of pizza or an ice cream cone can be part of their balanced lifestyle and do no harm.

Each of you reading this book has the opportunity to dodge this difficult roadblock to happiness. You are still young enough to remember your early years, when you didn't judge yourself. Take a stand; get physically connected and confident. You are lucky! It will be much easier for you now than it would be in 10 or 20 years. Don't wait. Don't say that you will start moving after high school or after college or after grad school or after you have been at your career a few years or after you have kids or once your kids go to school or when your kids graduate. The clock never stops running, for anyone. You will always have to make time; it will always be a juggle. Get used to juggling, and as you do, make sure that you prioritize movement.

The truth is that you will be a better student, achiever, and role model if you are physically available and empowered. You will process stress better and produce happy hormones, so that when the challenging days arise (and they always will), you will be naturally equipped to hit them head-on. The more you work your body, the more that you will become creative and clear. Stress is toxic. It always brings on self-judgment and a feeling of discomfort in our own skin, a lack of connection between mind and body that causes us to underperform in life, feel unhappy, and be prone to the onset of disease.

Many adult women have to chip through layers of calcified doubt before they can even start to feel good about moving again. But you have a unique opportunity to avoid all that extra work. This is why it's so great to be a teenager! You have a head start. You can bring your attention to the amazing machine that is your body before that connection fades away in a sea of insecurity. Make movement a consistent part of your life—every day—and reach adulthood with an already ingrained connection to your body. Your body is your ally in your search for a bright and balanced life.

BRUSH YOUR TEETH, WASH YOUR FACE, MOVE YOUR BODY

I wrote the CONNECT section of this book with the goal of inspiring you to listen deeply to the physical, mental, and emotional parts of yourself. In EAT, I encourage you to become a bold gatekeeper who determines what foods are granted entry to your body and what foods are left on the shelf—*we're talking to you, processed junk food*. Here, in MOVE, I ask you to take the final step toward living a life in balance by taking ownership of your movement.

We have been given the gift of bodies that are designed to move, not only to take us from point A to point B, but to keep our physical, mental, and emotional selves activated and healthy. Moving keeps your muscles lean, your bones strong, and your cardiovascular system at peak performance, and it also contributes to a healthy brain, a calm nervous system, and the fight against many diseases.

Movement is part of my everyday life. It's that simple. I do a focused workout every day because I know that movement keeps me healthy and in balance. I find time each day to get my workout in, regardless of how busy I am or how many people are vying for my attention. I encourage you, too, to become an advocate for your own movement, creating the time and space to get a focused workout 5 to 7 days a week for 30 to 50 minutes. This requires standing up for your own movement, telling yourself, and those in your life, if necessary: *I have to show up for my physical self because it is an absolutely necessary part of taking care of my health.*

I find that I often have to make an important clarification about movement to my adult clients: The first goal of exercise should not be about looking good. When your desire to work out—to move in a dedicated, focused way, almost every day of the week—comes from an understanding that movement is directly connected to health and wellness, it will be so much more impactful than if it comes solely from a longing to improve your appearance.

Think about your teeth. You brush your teeth every day because you know that keeping your teeth clean helps to prevent plaque and gum diseases like gingivitis (you did know that, right?). You don't

I work out every single day for at least 30 minutes (I aim for 50 minutes). I will take a day off from working out if I'm sick or traveling, but I do everything I can to get some movement into my day even if that means doing a quick workout in the airport or getting up a little earlier.

—Tracy

brush them only because you want teeth that could star in a toothpaste commercial. The fact that taking care of your teeth contributes to a pearly white smile is a fabulous perk.

This is how it goes with movement. Working out regularly will absolutely help you look your best, but I don't want your appearance to be the dominant force behind your desire to exercise. Moving your body in a focused way is amazing for your long-term health, but in the short term it also makes you feel better—right then and there. This near instant gratification is a great reason to work out, but it's often not the primary inspiration for moving. So many women approach working out from a place of vanity. When they do so, their dedication to making movement a part of their everyday lives—for the rest of their lives—starts to fade sooner than they would like. Looks are simply not enough of a motivator. When these women hit their ideal weight or give up on changing their appearance, working out becomes less of a priority and their health is then jeopardized.

Make it a goal to integrate focused workouts into your everyday life. Yes, you will become stronger if you work out regularly, and this newfound strength will help you feel more beautiful and confident, but daily exercise needs to first come from a place of health. Working out keeps your heart functioning at peak performance, which keeps cholesterol levels in check and heart disease at bay (currently the number one killer of women in the United States). It also keeps your bones strong; you'll be ahead of the curve if faced with osteoporosis or decreased bone density later in life. More and more studies are finding that regular workouts also help to keep your brain in tip-top shape, potentially warding off degenerative brain diseases like Alzheimer's.

The benefits of working out don't stop there! Regular exercise releases endorphins, hormones that promote happiness (yay!), reduce stress, and beat back depression. This is especially useful when you're navigating the emotional ups and downs of menstrual cycle moodiness and the shifts and changes of puberty. Have you noticed that it's tough to stay sad when you're briskly walking in nature or shaking your booty to your favorite song? Your happy hormones start pumping when you move your body. Moving regularly can help manage your moods, keeping your brain clear and ready for all that it has to take in—and give out—during middle school, high school, and beyond.

We are alive during one of the laziest decades in history. Technological advances like Wi-Fi, Amazon Prime, iPhones, and Netflix keep our eyes glued to the screen and our butts glued to the couch. Consequently, we are using our bodies and minds less than we ever have before. At the current rate of the obesity epidemic, by 2030, more than half of Americans will be obese. That's not far away! This health scare isn't your fault. The generations that came before you fell into a habit of moving as little as possible—the current reliance on technology has only made it worse—but you can break this pattern by taking back your right to move.

YOUR WORKOUTS: TIME WELL SPENT

You may already be dedicating a good chunk of your time to moving, especially if you participate in seasonal sports. Sports are great! They are an amazing part of growing up—they allow you to tap into healthy competition, to train your body and mind to take on new skills and abilities, and to foster a sense of community through practices and games. But stop-and-go sports—any kind of competitive sport from volleyball to pole vaulting—are not substitutes for your personal workouts, even if they include some conditioning exercises.

School sports usually don't require you to maintain a workout regimen outside of practice sessions, although professional athletes work out pretty much every day of the week that they are not playing a game or traveling, often more than once a day. They must work out consistently so the game itself is not about strength or endurance, but about the strategy and agility of the sport. Can you imagine if a tennis pro got winded running across the court or if an Olympic gymnast didn't have the strength to pull herself onto the uneven bars? A professional athlete has to work out every day so she can maintain the fundamental physical requirements that will allow her to keep her brain entirely in the game. If you play sports, you know the benefits of rigorously attending all the extra practice sessions. You can feel the difference on the field.

But even if you've never played a sport in your life, you can taste the joy that comes from moving your body regularly with focus. This section will show you how! At the end of MOVE, you'll find a series of fun workouts that I designed specifically for teens. You can practice a different one each day until you've run through them all. When you work out 5 to 7 days a week, movement becomes a habit you will carry with you for the rest of your life.

Working out 5 to 7 days a week may seem like a lot at first, but would you skip more than a day between showers? Would you skip a night of sleep? You maintain your hygiene by bathing every day; you stay rested by sleeping for 7 to 10 hours a night; and now you will attend to your physical health by working out most days of the week. The way to success is finding a consistent time during the day to get your workouts in. You may wake up 45 minutes early to work out before the school day starts, or you might get your workout in before you eat dinner at night. Understanding your unique biorhythms helps. Are you naturally more energetic in the morning? Or is the evening when you shine? Paying attention to how you feel throughout the day will give you this information.

You may be bringing workouts into your life again after a break or starting to consistently exercise for the first time. Either way, it's important to remember that fitness is for everybody regardless of your natural ability or current strength or endurance. The best thing about working out? You will get better simply by doing it. It's easy to watch an athlete like Simone Biles and beat yourself up for being so far away from her skill level. It's important to remember that she's an Olympic gymnast. She is at the absolute top of her game and has trained her entire life to get to this level.

You can also become an incredible athlete if that's what you are really determined to achieve. I never want a young person to watch someone perform, whether it's at the Olympics or a team championship at your school, and think, I could never do that. By staying connected to your body through regular workouts and continuously practicing what you love to do, you will excel. This doesn't guarantee that you'll make it to Olympic tryouts, but in the attempt to get there, you will push your body and mind to places they have never gone before and reach goals that you have never even thought of setting for yourself.

I know this because even though becoming a professional dancer was not a reality for me, my years and years of training in the dance world prepared my body, mind, and heart for the career path I would eventually take. Even if you don't have professional athletic aspirations, making movement a priority throughout your teens and into adulthood will give you a head start to becoming an active adult. Regular exercise will set you up to enjoy using your body for fun, whether you explore mountain climbing, biking, horseback riding, skiing, snowboarding, surfing, or any other physical activity.

A TOTAL WORKOUT: BODY AND MIND

I approach working out a bit differently than most. I don't believe it's possible to find balance by doing specific exercises like running or pushups that isolate certain parts of the body. I discovered this through years of medical research, studying professional athletes, noting changes in my own body, and working closely with thousands of women of all shapes, sizes, and fitness levels. All of this gathering of data helped me understand that the body responds better when it is treated as one entity instead of as a group of disparate parts. This is why I developed workouts that are not only about burning calories or getting a butt that looks a certain way—though that certainly can happen with enough focus and consistency—but about engaging the totality of each person. You won't see me encouraging anyone to do biceps curls one day and jog on the treadmill the next.

My workouts are full body, including the head. The totality of a person includes what's going on in the brain as well as the thighs or arms. I want the mind to be invited to this party, too, and working only the heart or a certain set of muscles doesn't stimulate your gray matter as much as a full-body workout with surprising twists and turns. When you engage in a physical practice like my workout routines, or in a yoga or Pilates class where the workout is about you challenging your body to move in new ways (as opposed to fitness programs that require the use of extensive gear or equipment), it requires your physicality to kick in gear, but you also need to use your brain to focus on what's happening. The goal is to activate the more than 600 muscles (600!) of your body as well as your cerebral stuff. These kinds of exercises actually create new neural pathways, or new ways of thinking, in your brain, which helps to keep it functioning at top condition as you age. When all of you is working together to optimize your workout, you receive a boost of health that is about so much more than changing the way you look.

FIERCE FOCUS

When working out becomes a regular part of your life, I'll bet that it also becomes a welcome part of your life. That's how it is for me. I use my exercise time to activate and strengthen my body, but also to process all that is

GET GROOVIN'

We are designed to react to music. It's in our DNA! Check out what happens if you play music in front of a toddler. Little kids are operating from pure instinct; they are not slowed down by insecurities or what-ifs (What if I look silly while I'm getting down?), so they usually start boogying the minute they hear the first note. My young daughter dances in supermarket aisles, on the playground, in her car seat—anywhere! Music is a huge part of my workouts, when I'm alone and when I'm teaching others, because it creates an irresistible current that helps to keep us motivated, activated, energized, and inspired. I use music to go deeper into my own focus. It helps me tune out outside voices and tap into my own inner reserves of strength.

Music gets our hips moving, and it speaks to us emotionally and mentally, too. Activating an emotional and mental response during a workout ensures that all pieces of you are being activated—your physicality, but also your heart and your brain. When a song has touched you, either with its lyrics, beat, or both, you find yourself singing along unconsciously. This is great and

a necessary part of your workout time.

I encourage you to make workout playlists full of songs that move you. No song is off-limits. I use music to speak to any emotion I may be feeling: joy, frustration, sadness, excitement, or loneliness. Luckily there is a song (or 12!) for every situation and emotion. My playlists include a wide range of music from hard-core rap, pop, hip-hop, ballads, R & B, bebop, country, and more. Mostly, I look for music that will get my adrenaline pumping. Adrenaline is the hormone that your body produces when you need to perform. It's what drives Beyoncé to sing and dance at a top level for 2 hours in a packed stadium. It's what propels an NFL quarterback to give his best throughout a 3-hour game. And it's what will support you as you move through a challenging workout.

My current top five workout songs are:

"Bad Liar" (Selena Gomez)

"Flashback" (Calvin Harris)

"Cool Girl" (Tove Lo)

"24K Magic" (Bruno Mars)

"Run Away with Me" (Carly Rae Jepsen)

happening in my life. My workout time is a filter that pulls out worries, stresses, fears, and anxieties. This is why I designed the workouts in this book, and the ones for my adult clients, too, as focused periods of movement. Focused movements are free from all distractions, including electronic devices—using a device to play music is the one exception. (You can read more about that in "Get Groovin'" above.) You give your full attention to moving your body.

When you focus on your fitness, you step into each workout knowing that you are entering a dedicated period of You Time. You won't be walking on the treadmill staring at the TV or checking your Instagram while you do lunges. That would pull your energy away from you. Moving your body with focus and intention transforms the movements into a way of connecting deeply with yourself. Here, you give your brain and heart an opportunity to work through any issues or challenges that they may be holding. It's a meditation of sorts that allows you to process anything and everything that's going on in your world, from conflict with a friend, a difficult class or assignment, or instability at home. I find that I often emerge from a workout inspired and uplifted from all the adrenaline and endorphins I produced while moving, but also calmer, more peaceful, and with a different perspective on a problem that I've been facing.

From what I remember from my own years as a teenager and what I see in my teenage son, a major part of getting through the years that bridge childhood and adulthood is understanding that you can influence the outcomes of many aspects of your life, but you'll never control them all. You can study for a test in hopes of getting a good grade; you can do all your chores in hopes of receiving your allowance; you can attend every softball practice in hopes of killing it at the big game. Yet sometimes the outcome doesn't match your effort. The test covered unexpected material; your mom wanted you to take the garbage out and clean the bathroom; you missed the fly ball. You're going to make mistakes. You're going to be disappointed. You're going to get hurt. The hard stuff is guaranteed, so it's important to factor in a method of working through your feelings so you can move forward and try again. You can always talk to a friend or family member or write in your journal, but there's nothing quite like sweating it out! It will be tempting to skip your daily workout when you're feeling down, but this is exactly when you should get moving. Feeling strong physically makes it easier to heal the hurt.

GET CURIOUS

Moving can feel intimidating, especially if you haven't done a whole lot of it recently (or ever). I understand how scary it can feel to ask your body to assume new shapes and to move in new ways. It's tempting to compare yourself to others and to tell yourself that you don't have what it takes. My adult clients experience feelings like this all the time, and I'm sure you do, too. The exciting news is that it doesn't matter if you played sports every day of your life before picking up this book or if you never set one foot on a track or a field. It doesn't matter if you consider yourself overweight or in shape, athletic or lethargic. Everything you've done before picking up this book—and everything you've thought—is in the past. Making the bold and brave decision to show up for your health and create a life that is truly in balance starts right now. I encourage every woman and every teen who wants to feel better in her body to start where she is today. You are exactly where you need to be.

Your best friends on this movement journey will be curiosity and awareness. Take curiosity with you as you begin to practice the workouts in this section, and the process will be a whole lot more fun. Keep curiosity with you as you dive deeper into working out, and you will discover aspects about yourself that will help your exercise time be more impactful: You will feel happier and stronger, and you will look healthier. Curiosity allows you to enter each workout with a light heart and an open mind. Before you start each workout, ask yourself a key question: *What is it going to feel like to move my body today?* That's curiosity. As you transition through each movement, notice what's happening in your body and mind without labeling it or judging it. That's awareness. A curious mind is open and neutral, simply interested in what's happening without labeling it as good or bad. I always say, "Don't judge me, don't judge the person next to you, and don't judge yourself. This is not a race. This is not a competition."

As you practice the exercises in this book, you may find that you are able to tear through all the exercises, or you may find that you are able to do only a few of the moves, or you may discover that you are unable to do any of the movements without getting tired right away. Whatever the result, treat it as valuable information—an awareness that will help you as you continue to show up for your workouts each day. It may be as simple as: *I'm aware that my arms get tired when I extend them for more than a few seconds. Or, I'm aware that all I ate today was a bagel with butter, and I'm feeling pretty lethargic now. Or, I'm aware that my legs feel strong during Cheerleading Act (page 126), but weaker during Tailgate Hindquarters (page 142).* You have to get curious to find the awareness, and once you have the information, you can take steps to grow and improve. Curiosity gives you the courage to ask: What is my range of motion in this movement? How strong am I? How flexible am I? Can I do all of the reps? It also gives you insight into your mental approach. You can ask: Do I make excuses when it gets hard? How much tolerance do I have for discomfort? How motivated am I?

Curiosity and awareness are at the heart of a Growth Mind-Set. When you approach life with a desire to grow, you acknowledge that you are currently at a certain level of experience, expertise, or skill, and you are willing and excited to do the work required to take you to the next level. This mind-set is especially useful when you begin integrating workouts into your daily life, because it actually takes a lot of time to become good at exercise. There are two steps to the

Don't judge me, don't judge the person next to you, and don't judge yourself. This is not a race. This is not a competition.

MOVE

FIVE THINGS TO PRACTICE

1 MAKE MOVEMENT A PART OF YOUR EVERYDAY LIFE
You brush your teeth every day to keep them healthy and looking clean and white. Now you will move your body every day so it remains healthy and looking strong and beautiful. It's that simple. Movement simply becomes part of your day.

2 TURN EVERY WORKOUT INTO A FOCUSED WORKOUT
Make your workout about you! Turn off the TV, put your phone down (unless it's playing music, of course), and bring your attention to your body and mind. Your workout time is your time—use it to process any hard emotions that you're experiencing and to feel strong and alive.

3 MEET YOUR BEST FRIENDS: CURIOSITY AND AWARENESS
Trade judgment for curiosity and awareness. Working out becomes a lot more fun when you approach each of your workouts with a curious mind, asking, I wonder what it's going to feel like to move my body like this today? Use awareness to note how your body and mind react to your workout. Where do you have room to grow?

4 TURN ON YOUR GROWTH MIND-SET
When you adopt a Growth Mind-Set, you acknowledge that you are currently at a certain level of experience, expertise, or skill, and you are willing and excited to do the work required to take you to the next level. A Growth Mind-Set will carry you anywhere you want to go. A Fixed Mind-Set will keep you stuck.

5 CREATE YOUR ULTIMATE WORKOUT PLAYLIST
The right tunes create an irresistible current that helps to keep you motivated, activated, energized, and inspired. Use music to go deeper into your focused workouts. Songs help you to block out outside voices and tap into your inner reserves of strength. Music also stimulates your heart and mind. Create playlists for different days and moods. Experiment with lots of genres, from rock to pop to jazz and hip-hop. No song is off-limits!

process. First, you learn how to do the movements. This is a practical, systematic approach requiring practice, patience, and determination. Second, you use curiosity and awareness to see how your unique body reacts to the movements. Where are you strong, and where are you weaker? This is where you refine your relationship to the practice and discover places to learn and grow. Remember, when it comes to your everyday workouts, you are accountable only to yourself. I want you to respect yourself enough to see where you can grow and push yourself to the best of your ability.

A Growth Mind-Set sets you up to accomplish anything you desire. A Fixed Mind-Set, on the other hand, keeps you stuck. When someone approaches working out from a fixed place, she may think, *I hate leg lifts, so I'm going to do only the bare minimum of three reps. Tomorrow I'll try to do three as well. Someone with a Growth Mind-Set thinks, These leg lifts are challenging! Let's see if I can do three. Tomorrow I'll see if I can do four.* A Fixed Mind-Set is dangerous because it does all it can to prevent you from growing. If you approach your workouts from a fixed place and don't see results—and you won't because you're not pushing yourself to grow—you'll likely come up with excuses for being stuck. You may tell yourself that nobody in your family is athletic; you may tell yourself that you've always been weak. Instead of approaching your current state of fitness with curiosity and using awareness to note the places where you have room to grow, you do all you can to keep yourself where you are. This is self-sabotage at its finest.

Throughout my 20-year career of supporting women in achieving their health and wellness goals, I have seen that a Growth Mind-Set leads to success more than any other technique—more than severe dieting or obsessive exercising. Women have beat obesity, recovered from severe health conditions, and cultivated strength and vitality by believing they can grow and change and pushing themselves to do so.

Integrating movement into your everyday life while you are young will ensure that fitness becomes an integrated part of your value system. Movement will be more than a trend you're exploring, even more than a habit you create— it will be a standard that you set for yourself. Did I brush my teeth? Check. Did I wash my face? Check. Did I work out? Check. When you do a focused workout at least 5 days a week, you are standing up for your health and making an unwavering decision to inspire your body (and mind and heart) to be the best it can be. Through movement you will find strength, endurance, and balance, and you will feel more beautiful, vibrant, and alive than you ever have.

Let's get moving!

FUNKY
FRESH
WORKOUT

To learn the lingo, check out the Vocabulary on page 210.

SIDE JAZZ ARMS

OPTIONAL EQUIPMENT:
3-pound hand weights

1 Stand with both arms straight out with jazz hands palms front.

2 Swing your arms on the diagonal with your working arm higher.

3 Return your arms to your sides.

4 Pulse your working arm straight back.

Repeat on the other side.

ARMS

DOUBLE DUTCH FLIPS

OPTIONAL EQUIPMENT:
3-pound hand weights

1 Hold your arms out to your sides with your palms facing up.

2 Lift your working arm slightly and flip your palm to face down.

3 Return.

4 Repeat on the nonworking arm.

5 Return.

6 Repeat lifting both arms simultaneously and flipping your palms down. Return.

LATERAL SIDE SWINGS

OPTIONAL EQUIPMENT:
3-pound hand weights

1 Hold your arms out to your sides with jazz hands palms front.

2 Swing your nonworking arm across your chest while dropping your working arm down by your side.

3 Return your arms to the starting position (arms held out to your sides).

4 Repeat on the other side. Keep your arms straight the whole time.

ARABESQUE LIFT TO HIP TAP

YOU'LL NEED:
1.5-pound ankle weights

1 Position yourself with both elbows on the floor, nonworking knee down, and nonworking leg straight back with your toe on the floor.

2 With your working leg, perform a straight arabesque lift up.

3 Return and lower your toe to the floor.

4 Invert/lean into your working hip, tapping it down as your working elbow lifts slightly.

FOURTH POSITION KICK

YOU'LL NEED: 1.5-pound ankle weights

1 Sit in fourth position with your working leg back and your elbow bent into your waist, with your nonworking hand on the floor.

2 Kneel up onto your nonworking knee and kick your working leg straight out to the side while reaching your working arm up.

3 Return to the sitting position.

4 Repeat.

{ MOVE } 65

CROSSED DOWN DOG PLANK

YOU'LL NEED: 1.5-pound ankle weights

1 Kneel forward with both hands down and your working leg in attitude back.

2 Press your nonworking leg to down dog plank position, extending your working leg to a crossed arabesque.

3 Kneel onto your nonworking knee as your working leg returns to attitude, then tiny pulse that leg in attitude.

BACK FACING BRIDGE

YOU'LL NEED: 1.5-pound ankle weights

1 Face back in a bridge position with your hips up high. Using your working arm for support, reach your nonworking arm up to the ceiling.

2 Flip to face down, kneeling onto your nonworking knee and placing both hands on the floor. Extend your working leg up to crossed arabesque.

3 Return to bridge without touching your working knee down.

LEGS

WRAP BACK ATTITUDE

YOU'LL NEED: 1.5-pound ankle weights

1 Position yourself with your body facing slightly into your nonworking corner, with your nonworking hand and knee down. Place your working hand on your hip and wrap your working leg back in a hip-height attitude position.

2 Extend your working leg to the side.

3 Return to the wrapped hip-height attitude position, slightly dipping your chest down.

LIFT TO SOUS-SUS

YOU'LL NEED: 1.5-pound ankle weights

1 Face forward on all fours. Lift your working leg back into attitude position and dip your chest.

2 Move your nonworking leg into a plank as you lower your working leg to sous-sus on top of your nonworking leg.

3 Return to the kneeling position.

4 Repeat.

ABS

PROPPED-UP SWING

YOU'LL NEED: 1.5-pound ankle weights

1 Lean back and prop yourself up on your working elbow, with your nonworking arm wrapped around your waist. The foot of your nonworking leg should be flat on the floor, with your knee bent up.

2 Swing your working leg open to the side, turning it out with a flexed foot. Cross it over your nonworking knee.

3 Return your leg to the side.

4 Repeat.

SIDE PLANK

YOU'LL NEED: 1.5-pound ankle weights

1 Get into a side plank balance with your nonworking arm down, your working arm reaching up to the ceiling, and both legs straight and stacked.

2 Reach your working arm down toward the floor while pulling in your abdominals to maintain a stable side plank position.

3 Return your arm to the starting position, reaching to the ceiling, and repeat.

ABS

KNEE PULL AND HOVER

YOU'LL NEED: 1.5-pound ankle weights

1 Lie on your back with your legs straight out and together. Hold your hands behind your head, which is resting on the floor.

2 Bring your working knee to your chest as you pull your abdominals in and lift your head toward your knee.

3 Extend your leg back down straight, keeping it lifted slightly off the floor and resting your head down.

4 Lift the same leg straight up with your toes toward the ceiling, pulling your abdominals in and lifting your head toward your leg.

5 Return your leg to a straight hover lifted slightly off the floor. Repeat on the other side.

URBAN DRILL

To learn the lingo, check out the Vocabulary on page 210.

ARMS DOWN, HEELS UP

OPTIONAL EQUIPMENT:
3-pound hand weights

1 Stand with your legs slightly turned out, your working heel lifted, and your arms extended out to the sides.

2 Bend your knees and lower your arms so that your palms face each other.

3 Return to standing position/arms up and repeat, keeping the working heel lifted the entire time. Do on the other side.

DO THE TWIST

OPTIONAL EQUIPMENT:
3-pound hand weights

1 Stand with your arms extended out to the sides with your palms facing up.

2 Rotate to face your palms down while lifting your arms slightly higher.

3 Return to the starting position and repeat.

FIFTH POSITION HIGH/LOW

OPTIONAL EQUIPMENT:
3-pound hand weights

1 Start with your arms in a rounded low fifth position with your palms facing up in front of your hips.

2 Keeping your arms in the same shape, lift them above your head, flipping your wrists so your palms face up and are flexed.

3 Lower your arms and repeat.

❶   ❷   ❸

LEGS

STACKED LEGS TO ARABESQUE

YOU'LL NEED: 1.5-pound ankle weights

1 Lie on your working hip with both elbows down and your legs stacked and bent.

2 Lift your working hip off the floor as your nonworking leg extends to arabesque and you shift forward.

3 Return to starting position and repeat.

HYDRANT PULL TO SIDE KICK

YOU'LL NEED: 1.5-pound ankle weights

1 Position yourself face forward, favoring your nonworking corner with your nonworking knee and elbow and your working hand down. Your working leg should be in a low hydrant pull forward.

2 Pull your working leg behind you and slightly up, keeping the bent position.

3 Extend/kick your leg to the side.

ARABESQUE TO ATTITUDE

YOU'LL NEED: 1.5-pound ankle weights

1 Kneel facing your nonworking side and pull your working knee toward your chest.

2 Extend back to a parallel arabesque as you extend your working leg to plank position.

3 Return down onto your working knee as you pull your nonworking knee to your chest again.

4 Lift your nonworking leg up to attitude back.

SIDE PLANK TO KICK FRONT

LEGS

YOU'LL NEED: 4-pound ankle weights

1 Face forward and get into a side plank with your head to your nonworking side and your nonworking hand supporting you. Reach your working arm up to the ceiling and put your legs in a straight stacked position.

2 Extend your working leg front by bending the leg first.

3 Return to stacked legs by bending the leg again and keeping your hips lifted and stable.

PLANK REACHES

YOU'LL NEED: 4-pound ankle weights

1   Face forward in plank position.

2   Reach forward, allowing your hips to shift in alignment with your arm.

3   Alternate arms and repeat.

WIDE DOWN DOG REACH

YOU'LL NEED: 4-pound ankle weights

1 Lie on your stomach with your nonworking leg straight and out to the side on the floor and your working leg straight and back on the floor, with your working toes tucked under and both hands down.

2 Pull in your abdominals to straighten your arms, push your hips up, and reach your working hand back through your legs.

3 Bring your working hand back down so that both arms are down and you're in a pushup/wide plank hover position.

4 Step your nonworking leg back across your working leg into fourth position, with your chest open and reaching your nonworking arm to the ceiling.

5 Return your nonworking leg to the nonworking side in a wide plank hover.

③

④

⑤

ABS

LEGS UP, BENT CRUNCH

YOU'LL NEED: 4-pound ankle weights

1 Lie on your back with your legs extended up in the air at a 90-degree angle. Use your hands to support your head, which is resting on the floor.

2 Bend your knees and pull in your abdominals to lift your head. Repeat.

WIDE V SWIPE CROSS OPEN

YOU'LL NEED: 4-pound ankle weights

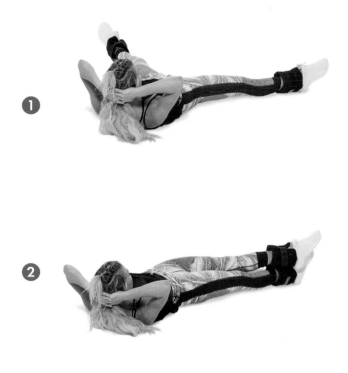

1 Lie on your back with your legs straight in a wide V position on the floor and your hands supporting your head in a slightly lifted position.

2 Swipe your working leg across to close over the opposite leg.

3 Swipe open to return to a wide V, but hovering slightly off the floor. Repeat.

ABS

WIDE V TAP, EXTEND UP

YOU'LL NEED: 4-pound ankle weights

1 Lie on your back with wide bent knees facing the ceiling, toes down on floor and hands supporting your head, which is resting on the floor.

2 Pull in your abdominals to lift your head up and simultaneously extend your working leg up to the ceiling.

3 Return your working toes to the floor, keeping the abdominal crunch.

4 Extend your nonworking leg up to the ceiling. Repeat.

GRAPHIC
DESIGN

To learn the lingo, check out the Vocabulary on page 210.

W ARMS

YOU'LL NEED: 3-pound hand weights

1 Stand with your arms bent in the air to the sides in a W position, palms facing front.

2 Close your arms together, maintaining the bent position.

3 Repeat.

ELBOW DOWN TO HIGH V

YOU'LL NEED: 3-pound hand weights

1 Stand with your nonworking arm extended up to the nonworking diagonal, palm facing out, and your working elbow pulled in toward your waist with the palm facing up.

2 Reach both arms up in a high V position with your palms facing out.

3 Pull your nonworking elbow down into your waist with the palm facing up.

4 Reach both arms up to a high V with your palms facing out. Repeat.

❶   ❷   ❸   ❹

SWIPE HIGH, BEND LOW

YOU'LL NEED: 3-pound hand weights

1 Start with both arms straight down on your nonworking side with your palms facing each other and close together.

2 Swipe your working arm straight up to the high working diagonal with your palms facing out.

3 Bend your working elbow to reach/extend back down to the nonworking low diagonal to repeat.

SIDE PLANK PASSÉ TO ARABESQUE

OPTIONAL EQUIPMENT:
1.5-pound hand weights

1 Get into a side plank position with your nonworking arm supporting your weight. Reach your working arm up to the ceiling and place your working knee in a parallel passé resting on the opposite leg.

2 Extend your working leg back to a slightly crossed arabesque.

3 Pull your working knee forward to return to passé.

4 Repeat, engaging your core and pressing your nonworking shoulder down the whole time.

LEGS

LUNGE, BRIDGE, LUNGE, ARABESQUE

OPTIONAL EQUIPMENT:
1.5-pound hand weights

1 Step forward on your working foot with your nonworking knee and hand down, and your working hand free.

2 Place your working hand down at your working side and step up onto your nonworking foot at your nonworking side, pressing your hips up to a bridge position and reaching your nonworking arm up to the ceiling.

3 Return to the original lunge with your nonworking shin and hand and your working foot down.

4 Extend your working leg back to arabesque as your working arm reaches forward in opposition.

LEGS

STEP UP TO CROSSED ARABESQUE

OPTIONAL EQUIPMENT:
1.5-pound hand weights

1 Facing your nonworking side, lunge onto your working foot with your nonworking knee and both hands down.

2 Step onto your working foot and lift your nonworking leg back into a crossed attitude position, straightening your working leg and slightly lifting your nonworking hand off the floor.

3 Return down to the lunge position to repeat.

STANDING COUPÉ EXTENSION

OPTIONAL EQUIPMENT:
1.5-pound hand weights

1 Stand upright on a naturally turned out, slightly bent working leg with the nonworking leg bent behind in a coupé position and your arms down in a low fifth position.

2 Lean your torso forward and extend your nonworking leg to parallel side, straightening the supporting leg and reaching your arms outside to second position.

3 Lift your torso to stand upright and return to plié coupé to repeat.

① ② ③

DOWN DOG SPLIT

YOU'LL NEED: 1.5-pound ankle weights

1 Face toward your nonworking side in down dog split with your nonworking leg extended up in a high arabesque.

2 Bend your nonworking leg through to sit onto your nonworking hip with your nonworking leg tucked under and your working leg hovering straight out to the side. Your nonworking hand should be down at your nonworking side, and your working hand down in front of your torso.

3 Keeping your nonworking arm straight, slide down onto your nonworking side while extending your working leg straight up to the ceiling and extending your nonworking leg straight out toward the working side staying down on the floor.

4 Return up to seated position with your working leg straight and hovering slightly off the floor.

5 Stand onto your working foot and extend your nonworking leg up into down dog split.

FOURTH POSITION STEP BACK

YOU'LL NEED: 1.5-pound hand weights

1 In a high fourth position, balance on your nonworking shin with your nonworking hand down at your nonworking side and your working toes stepped behind your nonworking shin, keeping the heel up and your hips hovering off the floor.

2 Turn to face your nonworking side with both hands down as you lower your chest toward the floor and extend your working leg up to arabesque.

3 Step your working foot back to return to the starting position and repeat.

LEANING BACK KNEE PULL

YOU'LL NEED: 1.5-pound ankle weights

1 Lie back on the nonworking diagonal propped up on your nonworking elbow, with your nonworking knee bent/tucked in, your working hand on your hip, and your working leg up in the air in a bent attitude side position.

2 Extend your working leg straight toward the working diagonal, hovering it slightly off the floor.

3 Pull in your abdominals to lift your working knee back toward your working shoulder and repeat.

ABS

SIT UP, ROLL DOWN

YOU'LL NEED: 1.5-pound ankle weights

1 Lie down on your back with both legs on the floor and straight together, stretching your abdominals by reaching your arms back over your head on the floor.

2 Pull in your abdominals to round your back and roll up to sit up tall, reaching your arms up to the ceiling.

3 Round your back and stretch forward, reaching your arms toward your toes and resting your torso forward over your legs and stretching your lower back.

4 Sit up tall and reach up again.

5 Pull in your abdominals to roll down through your spine one vertebra at a time to lie back down, reaching your arms back over your head after lying down. Each move gets one count.

ABS

PLANKING SHIN DROP

YOU'LL NEED: 1.5-pound ankle weights

1 Position your working leg back in a plank with both hands on the floor and drop/tap your nonworking shin down slightly inverted (with the knee in and toes out) onto the floor.

2 Pull in your abdominals to lift and extend your nonworking leg to the back nonworking diagonal, keeping it parallel and at hip height as you balance on your hands and working foot.

3 Return your nonworking shin back down to the inverted starting position and repeat.

1

2

3

OUT OF THIS WORLD SCULPTING

To learn the lingo, check out the Vocabulary on page 210.

EGYPTIAN ARMS REACH

YOU'LL NEED: free arms with no hand weights

1 Stand with your arms lifted out to the sides in an Egyptian or W position with flexed hands higher and bent elbows lower.

2 Close your working arm across your body until it's next to your opposite arm, maintaining bent elbows and flexed wrists.

3 Return to the starting position.

4 Extend your working arm straight out to the working side, keeping the palm facing up. Bend your working elbow to return to the starting position and repeat.

RIB CAGE DANCE

YOU'LL NEED: free arms with no hand weights

1 Stand with your arms bent parallel in front of your torso and palms facing each other at eye level.

2 Isolate your rib cage by pulling it back and then toward the working side, looking in that direction and flipping your working palm in and your nonworking palm out.

3 Return your torso back to center with both palms facing in.

4 Alternate sides and repeat.

DIAGONAL HAND SLIDE

YOU'LL NEED: free arms with no hand weights

1 Stand with your feet wide, knees slightly bent, and both hands touching your nonworking hip.

2 Slide your hands down your nonworking leg.

3 Touch your nonworking outer ankle.

4 Slide your hands back up your leg to your nonworking hip.

5 Extend and reach your arms to a wide open diagonal with your working arm high and your nonworking arm low and your fingers spread open. Alternate sides.

SHOULDER STAND TO HIGH ARABESQUE

YOU'LL NEED: 4-pound ankle weights

1 Rest in a shoulder stand on your working shoulder with your working arm straight out and the palm facing up, your nonworking hand down, your working cheek down, your working knee down, and tap inverted nonworking knee down on floor.

2 Extend your nonworking leg up to a high arabesque.

3 Return down and repeat. Engage your abdominals the entire time to maintain balance in the shoulder stand.

❶

KNEE HOVER

YOU'LL NEED: 4-pound ankle weights

1 Place your nonworking elbow, nonworking knee, and working hand on the floor, with your working knee hovering slightly off the floor in a parallel bent position.

2 Extend your working leg straight out to the working side, leaning in opposition into the nonworking hip. Return and repeat.

COUPÉ SWING INTO ATTITUDE

YOU'LL NEED: **4-pound ankle weights**

1 Kneel forward with your nonworking leg and both hands on the floor, working leg in coupé swing behind your nonworking knee.

2 Lift your working leg back in attitude position.

3 Lower and lift to repeat.

FLEXED KNEE PULL TO ARABESQUE

YOU'LL NEED: 4-pound ankle weights

1 Kneel forward with your nonworking knee and both hands on the floor, and pull your working knee forward wider than hip-width apart with a flexed foot.

2 Extend your working leg up to arabesque while maintaining a flexed foot and bending your elbows slightly to accommodate the height of your leg.

3 Lower to the starting position and repeat.

CROSSED-BACK LUNGE TO ARABESQUE

YOU'LL NEED: 4-pound ankle weights

1 Kneel forward with your nonworking shin and both hands on the floor, with your working leg straight in a crossed-back lunge on the floor on the nonworking back diagonal.

2 Bend your knee and extend your working leg straight up to arabesque, slightly bending your elbows to accommodate the height of your leg.

3 Keep your leg straight to return back down to the lunge position and repeat.

HYDRANT REBOUND

YOU'LL NEED: 4-pound ankle weights

1 Facing your nonworking side with your nonworking knee and both hands on the floor, pull your working knee forward in a hydrant position, slightly dipping your chest and pulling in your abdominals.

2 Rebound your working leg, transitioning through a back attitude position.

3 Extend/kick your working leg straight and high to the working side, pulling in your working side abdominals and lifting your working hand off the floor. Transition your leg through back attitude to return to the starting position and repeat.

PLANK WALKS

YOU'LL NEED: 4-pound ankle weights

1 In plank position, step your nonworking leg across and under the working leg.

2 Transfer your weight into your nonworking foot and hands and extend the working leg back toward the back working diagonal.

3 Step your working leg under and across the nonworking leg, maintaining the plank position by engaging your abdominals.

4 Transfer your weight into your working foot and hands and extend your nonworking leg to the back nonworking diagonal. Alternate and repeat.

ABS

KNEE TO NOSE

YOU'LL NEED: 4-pound ankle weights

1 Lie down on your back with your legs straight out on the floor in fifth position with your working leg on top and your hands supporting your head, which is resting on the floor.

2 Pull in your abdominals to lift your head and working knee up in attitude position, pulling your knee to your nose.

3 Lower to repeat.

SIDE LYING SWIPE

YOU'LL NEED: 4-pound ankle weights

1 Lying on your nonworking side with your nonworking leg tucked and your nonworking bent arm supporting your head, pull in your abdominals to hover your working leg slightly off the floor in a bent front attitude position on the nonworking side and reach your working arm back toward your working side.

2 Lift your working leg in a long, high side attitude position, rounding your back and pulling in your abdominals to reach your working arm forward toward the nonworking side in opposition.

3 Pull/swipe your working leg across your body to return to the starting position and repeat.

CHEER-LEADING ACT

To learn the lingo, check out the Vocabulary on page 210.

JAZZ HANDS TO OPEN

YOU'LL NEED: free arms with no hand weights

1 Stack your hands (with your fingers spread wide) over your head.

2 Lower your hands down to your belly.

3 Open your hands to the sides, keeping your elbows bent.

① ② ③

EGYPTIAN ARMS UP

YOU'LL NEED: free arms with no hand weights

1 Hold your arms out to the sides bent with your palms facing up and flexed wrists.

2 Straighten your arms and lower them down with your palms pressing back. Alternate.

BENT PULSE/STRAIGHT PULSE

YOU'LL NEED: free arms with no hand weights

1 Hold both arms out to your sides.

2 Bend your working elbow, pulse it back, and return.

3 Straighten your arm, pulse it back, and return. Repeat on the opposite side.

ARABESQUE TAP CHEST

YOU'LL NEED: 1.5-pound ankle weights

1 Face your working corner, with your working hand and knee down and your nonworking arm reaching up behind.

2 Hold your nonworking leg up in a hip-level arabesque as your working hand quickly lifts off the floor to tap your chest.

3 Return your hand to the floor with a small pulse upward of your nonworking leg and then return to a hip-level arabesque.

3

HEADSTAND TO CROSSED ARABESQUE

YOU'LL NEED: 1.5-pound ankle weights

1 Place your head down on the floor, with your working hand down closer to your head and your nonworking hand down further to the side.

2 Move your working leg in a parallel knee pull to your chest and then extend up high in a crossed arabesque.

DIAMOND TO EXTENDED ARABESQUE

YOU'LL NEED: 1.5-pound ankle weights

1 Face your working side with your nonworking elbow and working hand on the floor, and your nonworking knee down with the working shin and foot up.

2 Place your working leg in attitude with the foot in diamond position on top of your nonworking foot. Stretch your working hand out to the side.

3 Twist your hips back and tap your working foot and nonworking outer shin down behind you, then return to your nonworking knee, extending your working leg up to arabesque.

HYDRANT PULL TO PLANK ARABESQUE

YOU'LL NEED: 1.5-pound ankle weights

1 Face your working diagonal with your nonworking knee and both hands on the floor.

2 Lift your hips and pull your working leg forward to a hydrant position, while planking your nonworking leg.

3 Extend your working leg up to arabesque.

FOURTH POSITION SIDE HOP SWITCH

YOU'LL NEED: 1.5-pound ankle weights

1 Face front on all fours and swing your working leg back through small attitude.

2 Pull both legs down to sit in fourth position.

3 Then kick to the side, lifting up onto your nonworking shin.

4 Sit back down into fourth position, jumping slightly to switch your legs to the opposite side. Keep your hands down.

5 Kick your opposite leg out to the side, and then return to facing front on all fours. Repeat starting on the other side.

{ MOVE }   137

FOURTH POSITION HAND TAP

YOU'LL NEED: 1.5-pound ankle weights

1 Place your nonworking shin parallel to the floor with the ball of your working foot behind in fourth position, with your working arm reaching up to the ceiling and your chest facing the working diagonal.

2 Lift your nonworking shin forward in a turned-out attitude and tap your working hand to your foot.

3 Return to the starting position and circle your arm back while slightly dipping your hips. Keep your nonworking hand and the ball of your working foot down the whole time.

WORKING HEEL STRETCH

YOU'LL NEED: 4-pound ankle weights

1 Lie down on your back, holding your head with your nonworking hand. Grab your working heel, stretching your leg toward your working shoulder.

2 Pull your nonworking knee to your chest.

3 Extend your nonworking knee straight forward, slightly hovering off the floor.

{ MOVE } 139

ABS

PLANK WITH HYDRANT PULL

YOU'LL NEED: 4-pound ankle weights

1 Place your nonworking leg in a plank position with both hands down and pull your working leg forward in a bent hydrant position.

2 Place both knees down on the floor, keeping your feet up.

3 Lower your chest down, hovering slightly off the floor with bent elbows.

4 Pull in your abdominals and push your chest up as you straighten your elbows.

PLANK DOWN, PLANK UP

ABS

YOU'LL NEED: 4-pounds ankle weights

1 Hold plank position.

2 Lower to one elbow.

3 Then, lower to other elbow.

4 Straighten first arm.

5 Then, straighten other arm, returning to plank position.

TAILGATE HIND-QUARTERS

To learn the lingo, check out the Vocabulary on page 210.

PULSE BACK TO OPEN DIAGONAL

YOU'LL NEED: 3-pound hand weights

1 Stand holding weights in front of your chest with your arms bent in first position, palms facing in.

2 Pulse your elbows back, keeping them lifted.

3 Return your arms to first position.

4 Open your arms to a wide diagonal stretch with your working arm higher/ nonworking arm lower, palms facing down and bending at your waist on the nonworking side.

5 Standing upright, close your arms to first position again and alternate sides.

①

②

③

④

⑤

BENT ARMS FLIP

YOU'LL NEED: 3-pound hand weights

1 Hold the weights up in a high V position above your head.

2 Bend your elbows, keeping them at shoulder level, and flip the weights down with your palms facing back and slightly round your back by engaging your abdominals.

3 Flip the weights up so your palms face front, raising your hands higher than your elbows. Your torso should come upright. Alternate and repeat.

1   2   3

LOW V, HIGH V, CRUNCH IN

YOU'LL NEED: 3-pound hand weights

1 Hold the weights straight up to the ceiling with your palms facing front.

2 Lower your arms straight down to a low V position at your sides with your palms facing in.

3 Lift your arms straight up to a high V position with your palms facing front.

4 Bend your arms in front of your chest with your palms facing in.

5 Pull your elbows down to your waist while slightly pulling in your abdominals.

CROSSED KNEES FLIP TO PLANK SWIPE

YOU'LL NEED: 1.5-pound ankle weights

1 Sit facing forward leaning back on your forearms with your working leg extended straight and your nonworking foot down and the knee pointing to the ceiling. Swipe your working leg open toward the working side with your leg turned out and your foot flexed.

2 Cross your working knee over your nonworking knee.

3 Open the working leg to the side again.

4 Pull in your abdominals to swipe your working leg across and flip toward the nonworking side on the nonworking elbow, with your hips slightly lifted off the floor.

5 Flip to face back with your nonworking knee/ elbow and working hand down, keeping your working knee off the floor.

6 Extend your nonworking leg to plank as your working leg does a slightly lifted parallel side swipe. Reverse roll back and repeat, always keeping the working knee off the floor.

LEGS

LEGS

SWING BACK TO BALANCED ARABESQUE

YOU'LL NEED: 1.5-pound ankle weights

1 Face front with your head to your nonworking side while sitting on your nonworking hip, with your nonworking elbow and working hand on the floor. Swing your working leg back in attitude.

2 Pull in your abdominals to swing your working leg forward and press your hips up as you flip over toward your nonworking side.

3 Kneel facing your nonworking side onto your nonworking elbow and your working hand.

4 Extend your nonworking leg up in a crossed arabesque and reach your nonworking arm up to the ceiling. Lower onto your nonworking knee and hip to roll back to the starting position and repeat.

TWIST ROLL TO TAP

YOU'LL NEED: 1.5-pound ankle weights

1 Kneel forward on your nonworking knee and elbow and your working hand, with the toes of your working foot tucked under.

2 Twist toward your nonworking side to face back and tap your working hip down with your nonworking hand free. Reverse the roll to return to the starting position and repeat.

STANDING BALANCE TO COUPÉ PLIÉ

YOU'LL NEED: 1.5-pound ankle weights

1 Face forward, standing on a slightly bent nonworking leg with your working leg bent behind in a low coupé position and your arms reaching out to the sides.

2 Slightly lean your torso forward over your nonworking leg and extend your working leg up toward the working side, bending your nonworking arm to help with balance. Lower your working leg to return to coupé and repeat.

BALANCED HYDRANT TO ARABESQUE DIP

YOU'LL NEED: 4-pound ankle weights

1 Balancing on your nonworking knee and hand, pull your working leg forward bent up in a hydrant position.

2 Place your working elbow on the floor and extend your working leg back in a high arabesque position, lowering your chest toward the floor.

3 Lift up into balancing hydrant pull to starting position and repeat.

CROSSED ARABESQUE PULSES

YOU'LL NEED: 4-pound ankle weights

1 Kneel forward on your nonworking knee with your hands wide apart and your working leg up in a crossed arabesque position just above hip height.

2 Pulse your leg up higher, dipping your chest as needed to accommodate the height of the leg.

3 Lower and lift your leg to repeat, keeping it straight the whole time.

ABS

ARMY ROLL TO SINGLE LEG PLANK AND SWIPE

YOU'LL NEED: 1.5-pound ankle weights

1 Lie on your back with your hands on your chest.

2 Roll toward your nonworking side onto your stomach, placing your hands down under your shoulders and tucking the toes on your nonworking foot under.

3 Pull in your abdominals and press up into plank position with your nonworking leg as your working leg swipes toward the working side, staying straight. Reverse to roll back and repeat.

PIKE/TUCK TO CRUNCH

ABS

YOU'LL NEED: 1.5-pound ankle weights

1 Lie down on your back and pull your working knee to your chest, with your nonworking leg straight and hovering slightly off the floor, and your hands supporting your head, which is also slightly lifted off the floor.

2 Extend both legs together and up to the ceiling, pulling in your abdominals to lift your head higher.

3 Lower your working leg straight to hover slightly off the floor and pull your nonworking knee into your chest. Extend both legs up and together again and alternate and repeat, using your abdominals to control the action of your legs.

ABS

CRUNCH CROSS ATTITUDE

YOU'LL NEED: 1.5-pound ankle weights

1 Lie on your back with your nonworking leg straight down and your hands supporting behind your head, which is slightly lifted off the floor, and then pull your working leg across your body toward your nonworking side in a bent attitude position hovering slightly off the floor.

2 Roll onto your back with your working knee tucked to your chest and use your abdominals to lift your straight nonworking leg up to the ceiling, lifting your head slightly higher. Lower your legs to the starting position and repeat.

HIPPY HAPPY
PURSUIT

To learn the lingo, check out the Vocabulary on page 210.

ARMS SWIPE LOW V TO HIGH V

OPTIONAL EQUIPMENT:
3-pound hand weights

1 Lean slightly forward with your knees bent and pulse straight arms back by your hips in a low V position with your palms facing down.

2 Stand in a neutral position and bring your arms in front of your hips with the palms facing each other and almost touching.

3 Slightly arch your back and pulse straight arms up in a high V position with your palms facing front.

① ② ③

PUNCH TO THE SKY, PUNCH TO THE SIDE

YOU'LL NEED: 3-pound hand weights

1 Holding 3-pound weights, stand with your elbows bent and your palms facing forward.

2 Extend your working arm straight up to the ceiling with your palm facing front and slightly lean your torso to the nonworking side, bending your elbow to your hip with an upright torso.

3 Extend your working arm straight out to the side, twisting it so the palm faces back with a slight lean.

4 Return your elbow to your hip with the palm facing front and stand upright.

REACH BOTH UP, REACH BOTH SIDE

YOU'LL NEED: 3-pound hand weights

1 Holding 3-pound weights, extend both arms straight up to the ceiling with your palms facing in.

2 Bend your elbows to lower your hands to your chin.

3 Extend both arms out to your sides with the palms facing down.

4 Return to the bent-elbows position with your palms facing in.

PLANK WITH SMALL KNEE LIFT AND ARABESQUE

YOU'LL NEED: 4-pound ankle weights

1 Get down on all fours and plank your working leg, keeping your nonworking shin down.

2 Lift your nonworking leg out to the side in a small turned-out attitude position.

3 Return your nonworking knee to the floor.

4 Lift and extend your working leg up through attitude.

5 Extend your working leg out and up to arabesque. Bend elbows if necessary to get more height in your working leg.

LEGS

LEGS

COUPÉ SWING INTO DIAGONAL

YOU'LL NEED: 4-pound ankle weights

1 Kneel forward on your nonworking knee, elbow, and working hand. Cross your working leg so it hovers slightly over your nonworking knee.

2 With your working leg perform a coupé swing in behind your nonworking knee.

3 Extend it up to the open diagonal through attitude.

①

②

③

FROGGY FEET LIFT TO WIDE PLANK PUSHUP

YOU'LL NEED: 4-pound ankle weights

1 Lie forward on your stomach with your legs bent and your feet together in froggy position, with both hands down and your elbows bent.

2 Lift/pulse both feet up, slightly lifting your thighs off the floor.

3 Place your feet on the floor in a wide plank.

4 Engage your abs to straighten your arms for a pushup.

5 Bend your arms and return back down.

{ MOVE } 169

LEGS

PARALLEL SIDE SHINS WITH LIFT BACK

YOU'LL NEED: 4-pound ankle weights

1 Kneeling forward on all fours, slightly lift both feet.

2 Twist your feet to your nonworking side, placing them down with parallel knees facing your working side.

3 Adjust your working shin straight back and lift your nonworking leg up to attitude back.

STRAIGHT SWING FRONT TO ARABESQUE

YOU'LL NEED: 4-pound ankle weights

1 Kneel forward on all fours. With a flexed foot, swing your working leg out straight to your front working corner while lifting your working hand slightly off the floor and slightly leaning into your nonworking hip.

2 Place both hands on the floor and swing your straight leg back and up through arabesque to crossed arabesque.

3 Lower your chest and bend your elbows to lift your working leg higher.

LUNGE TAP TO KICK SIDE

YOU'LL NEED: 4-pound ankle weights

1 Get into a high lunge with your working leg out to the side.

2 With your working hand on your hip, reach your nonworking arm across to tap the floor by your working foot.

3 Move your nonworking arm to your nonworking side and extend your working leg up to high parallel side as your working arm reaches to a high V position.

LEGS

WIDE PLANK CROSSED KNEE PULLS

YOU'LL NEED: 4-pound ankle weights

1 Get into a wide plank position.

2 Pull one knee across the center of your body toward the opposite elbow.

3 Return to the wide plank position.

4 Pull your other knee across the center of your body toward the opposite elbow.

ABS

PLANK WALKS

YOU'LL NEED: 4-pound ankle weights

1 Get into a plank position.

2 Pull one knee to your chest while keeping your other leg planked.

3 Switch legs.

4 Return to the plank position.

LUNGE TO PLANK

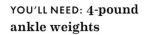

YOU'LL NEED: 4-pound ankle weights

1 Lunge with your working foot forward, your nonworking hand on the floor, and your working arm reaching up.

2 Move to a plank position.

3 Switch to lunge on the other side.

4 Return to a plank position.

APPENDIX

MEAL PLANS AND RECIPES

Here are some resources I love that you'll find helpful when following the meal plan. You can research each of these brands online and find what stores near you carry them. What's great about this process is that you will learn how to choose healthy foods, where to shop, and important key words to look for such as *organic*. I understand that these products are a bit more expensive, so please ask for your parents' support in stocking your home with a few or all of these options. If getting these exact products isn't possible, use common sense to make choices that are best for your health. If you're reaching for a real apple over a fast-food apple pie, we are headed in the right direction!

MY SUPERSTAR TEEN SHOPPING LIST

Instead of Doritos or Cheetos, here are some amazing options that I promise taste just as good. I am a real foodie! I love sweets, salty, savory—you name it—and the below choices really hit the spot!

BREAD
- Food for Life Ezekiel 4:9 Organic Bread (This is my favorite for toast and sandwiches.)

CEREALS
- Annie's (Frosted Oat Flakes, Cocoa Bunnies, Berry Bunnies)
- Kashi organic cereals

CHOCOLATE
- Green & Black's Organic Milk Chocolate
- Alter Eco Dark Velvet Organic Chocolate
- Enjoy Life Boom Choco Boom Chocolate Bars: Dark Chocolate, Ricemilk Crunch, or Ricemilk Chocolate flavors

CONDIMENTS
- Soy-Free Vegenaise
- Organic Dijon mustard
- Organic yellow mustard
- Sir Kensington Mayonnaise (I use the Sriracha or Chipotle varieties for extra flavor.)

FROZEN FOODS
- Trader Joe's Premium Salmon Burgers
- Ian's Gluten-Free Organic Frozen Chicken Patties
- Applegate Organic Gluten-Free Chicken Nuggets

LUNCHMEAT
- Applegate Herb Turkey Breast
- Applegate Oven Roasted Chicken Breast
- Applegate Roast Beef

PASTA
- Ancient Harvest (My favorite! It's gluten-free and organic. My daughter loves their Pow! protein pastas. My son's favorite is the Garden Pagodas quinoa variety.)

PASTA SAUCE
- Newman's Own Organics Tomato & Basil

PIZZA
- Against the Grain Three Cheese

SALAD DRESSING
- Newman's Own Organics Italian
- Organic Girl (These salad dressings are amazing. Choose your favorites.)

SNACKS
GARDEN OF EATIN' CHIPS
Favorite Flavors:
- Nacho Cheese (tastes like Doritos!)
- Chili & Lime
- Guac-A-Mole
- Yellow, White, Blue, or Red Tortilla Chips

BEARITOS PUFFED SNACKS
Favorite Flavors:
- Cheddar Puffs
- Veggie Puffs

FARMHOUSE CULTURE CHIPS
Favorite Flavors:
- Dill Pickle
- Sea Salt
- White Cheddar

EDEN FOODS POCKET SNACKS (1 OUNCE)
Favorite Flavors:
- Tamari Almonds
- Pistachios
- Pumpkin Seeds
- Dried Cherries, Blueberries, Cranberries, or the Quiet Moon mix

TUNA
- Wild Planet
- Safe Catch Elite (Note: Low mercury brands are very important!)

TRACY'S TIPS

Choose organic whenever possible. The most important word I want you to use across the board with the below menus is organic. From eggs to milk to chocolate to fruits and veggies, if you have the opportunity to purchase organic, please do; it's always better to choose foods in their natural states, free from pesticides and chemicals. If your budget or options won't allow you to purchase organic varieties of everything, prioritize buying organic versions of fruits and veggies that don't have a thick skin to protect themselves from chemicals. Here are some examples:

- Apples
- Berries
- Dairy
- Leafy greens
- Rice
- Tomatoes

Make cooking a family activity. Ask your parents to get involved in helping you in the kitchen. It is super easy to put fish on a baking sheet with a little avocado oil spray, lemon juice, and capers.

Choose low-mercury fish. Anytime I list fish on the menu, please make sure that you or your parents ask for a low-mercury fish. Here are some examples of low-mercury seafood:

- Anchovies
- Atlantic mackerel
- Rainbow trout
- Salmon
- Sardines
- Shrimp
- Tilapia
- Pacific sole

Take a tea break. Hot tea is a better habit to learn to enjoy than coffee, and there are so many fun flavors from brands like Yogi—even cinnamon vanilla.

Get chopping! It is so much easier to make a salad than you think, and fresh salads make a great packed lunch. Look for a reusable "on-the-go" container that will keep salads cool and fresh with an ice pack, and pack your dressing in a separate container so your salad stays crisp.

Go for squeaky clean. Always make sure to thoroughly wash fresh produce.

Pack a trio. There are three things that you need to learn to always have with you each day:

1 **WATER.** It is so important to hydrate primarily with water and to always have it on hand with you.

2 **A SNACK.** Whether you're headed to school or sports practice, or just hanging with friends, always make sure that you have a snack pack

with you. This is a habit that is extremely important to develop. Otherwise, you'll find yourself sliding in your nutrition purely because you aren't prepared and are "forced" into vending machine junk that is terrible for your brain, mood, skin, and weight. If you can get a hold of Eden Foods Pocket Snacks, I love them. My son's favorite is the Eden Tamari Almond snack pack. If you don't have those, you can put some almonds in a resealable plastic bag for when you're on the go. You could even take a bag of some of the chips mentioned above or a Justin's Classic Almond or Peanut Butter packet. An organic string cheese, an apple with a protein like almond butter, or a banana with organic peanut butter are also good choices.

3 **A CHOCOLATE BAR.** You should also always have your own candy bar on you in case you need to have a bit of sugar on the go. As a teenager, you are growing and burning a lot of energy. You will crave sugar, so make sure you're reaching for the right kind. My son likes the Green & Black's Organic Milk Chocolate bars the best. I have listed my favorites on page 178. It's not about never having a candy bar—it's about the quality and kind of candy bar you're putting into your system. In case you need something sweet throughout the day while your classmates may be eating Twinkies, you won't totally miss out—but you will be missing out on the added carbs and processed ingredients of other sweet snacks.

MEAL PLAN

I really believe in being able to make your own food choices as opposed to any-one telling you what you have to eat every day. I have laid out many choices in the form of individual days for breakfast, lunch, dinner, and desserts, but you can choose one from each category every day. Feel free to pick and mix what-ever days you would like since listening to your body's needs always comes first. Some days or weeks you may be craving more carbs than others. It is important to listen to that, but to also be balanced. If you love pasta, then your emotional self may make your body believe that it needs pasta 7 days a week for lunch and dinner—but that would be out of balance for your physical self.

MONDAY

Breakfast

Easy Eggs: Crack 2 eggs into a bowl and whip until combined. Melt a small amount of organic butter in a small skillet over low heat. Add the eggs and cook until nearly cooked through. Sprinkle shredded mozzarella in the pan and put a handful of spinach on top. Fold into an omelet, flip it, or scramble it. I love a little sea salt on top.

Lunch

Easy Turkey Sandwich: 2 slices of Ezekiel bread; as much turkey as you like; a few leaves of romaine lettuce; sliced tomato; Vegenaise; and 2 slices of provolone cheese

Dinner

Baked Fish in Lemon Caper Sauce with Zucchini and Onion Rice: In a saucepan, sauté sliced zucchini and chopped onion in a little organic rice wine vinegar. Boil rice in a separate saucepan. When the rice is done, add it to the zucchini mixture along with some low-sodium soy sauce.

Meanwhile, place the fish on a baking sheet coated with cooking spray. Top with lemon juice and capers to taste. Bake at 375°F until it flakes easily with a fork. Serve the rice mixture alongside the fish.

TUESDAY

Breakfast

Morning Smoothie: In a blender, combine a handful of frozen mango chunks, a handful of frozen strawberries, and a handful of frozen banana slices with a scoop of vanilla yogurt and enough vanilla rice milk to reach desired consistency. Blend and go.

Lunch

Chopped Salad: The night before making this salad, hard-cook an egg and put it in the fridge. The next morning, chop equal parts iceberg lettuce and red lettuce and put in a to-go container. Add sliced cucumber, sliced scallions, and broccoli florets (take a raw broccoli crown and shave off the florets from the top). Chop 2 string cheese sticks and add them to the salad. Either take the hard-cooked egg and eat it on the side or peel it and chop it into the salad. (You may want to wait to put it in the salad if you are taking it on the go.) Separately pack some Newman's Organic Italian Dressing to drizzle over the top.

Dinner

Pow! Pasta with Tomato Sauce: Cook and drain the pasta according to package directions. Meanwhile, in a saucepan, heat jarred organic tomato sauce with some fresh garlic and olive oil. In a skillet coated with some cooking spray or a bit of olive oil, sauté some chopped yellow onion, garlic, and Broccolini until tender. Mix the tomato sauce with the pasta and serve the veggies on the side.

WEDNESDAY

Breakfast
1 cup of oatmeal with honey

Lunch
Grilled Chicken with a Side Salad: Chop cucumber and tomato and combine with spinach. Crumble some feta cheese over the top and add dressing. Serve the grilled chicken on top or on the side.

Dinner
4 Corn Tortillas with Shredded Cheese: Place the tortillas in a warm skillet and cook, turning once, until warmed through on each side. Place shredded cheese over 2 of the tortillas. Cover each with the remaining tortillas and cook, turning once, until the cheese is melted. Serve with guacamole and pico de gallo (homemade or store-bought).

THURSDAY

Breakfast
Quick A.M. Chocolate Smoothie: In a blender, combine chocolate almond milk, frozen banana slices, and Greek yogurt with chocolate (you can find Greek yogurt cups that come with chocolate like FAGE Crossovers or Chobani Flip, or you can add a sprinkling of chocolate chips to whatever Greek yogurt you have). Blend to desired consistency.

Lunch
Chopped Salad: In a bowl or container, combine chopped romaine, sliced cucumber, and chopped red onion. In a small bowl, mix 1 tablespoon Vegenaise with 1 tablespoon ketchup. Toss the dressing with the salad. Top with a chicken breast from a purchased rotisserie chicken.

Dinner
Grilled fish with purple rice and grilled zucchini

FRIDAY

Breakfast
Asparagus Omelet: Crack 2 or 3 eggs in a bowl and whip until combined. Melt a small amount of butter in a small skillet over low heat. Add the eggs and cook until nearly cooked through. Sprinkle with shredded mozzarella cheese and sautéed chopped asparagus tips. Carefully fold into an omelet, flip, or scramble with sea salt.

Lunch
Deli Sandwich: 2 slices of Ezekiel bread with mustard; sliced lunchmeat; sliced tomato; romaine lettuce; and soy-free Vegenaise; plus a side of preferred chips

Dinner
Baked chicken breast with fresh rosemary, olive oil, and lemon juice; sautéed Broccolini with lemon

SATURDAY

Breakfast
Gluten-free pancakes (I love Bob's Red Mill Gluten-Free Pancake Mix with a little maple syrup); side of raspberries, blueberries, or blackberries

Lunch
Quesadilla: Heat 2 gluten-free corn tortillas (Mission gluten-free are my favorite) in a skillet over low heat. Sprinkle 1 tortilla with shredded Horizon or Organic Valley cheese and top with the second tortilla. (If you would like, you could add precooked shredded chicken breast.) Cook until the cheese melts. Serve with chopped tomato, cilantro, white onion, and lime and salt on the side.

Dinner
Easy Chicken Soup: Pour two 8-ounce containers of Pacific Chicken Bone Broth into a saucepan. Add precooked chopped chicken breast and bring to a quick boil. Reduce the heat, add 2 handfuls of cooked fusilli pasta, rosemary, sea salt, 1 chopped carrot, and ½ chopped onion. Heat through. Add 1 handful of spinach and cook for 30 seconds, or until the spinach wilts. Serve with a side of toast and butter, too, if desired.

SUNDAY

Breakfast

Berries, Yogurt, and Honey: Combine plain Greek yogurt with blueberries, raspberries, and blackberries. Drizzle with a bit of honey. (It is important to learn to love the taste of plain Greek yogurt, too, and mixing it with berries and honey is a great way to sweeten the deal.)

Lunch

Chicken Nuggets: Applegate Organic Chicken Nuggets with dipping sauce (I love mixing ketchup with Vegenaise, or using a little mustard or honey). Make a side salad by combining a couple of handfuls of spinach, chopped red onion, chopped cucumber, feta cheese, and dressing.

Dinner

Grilled Fish with a Side of Roasted Fingerling Potatoes and Cauliflower: Spread out washed fingerling potatoes and cauliflower florets on a baking sheet and drizzle with olive oil. I love Jacobsen Salt Co.'s Infused Rosemary Salt with fresh rosemary on top. Roast at 425°F for 20 minutes. Serve alongside the fish.

MONDAY

Breakfast

Banana French Toast: In a blender, combine 1 banana, 3 eggs, and a splash of milk. Blend until the banana is pureed. Pour into a bowl. Melt a dab of butter in a skillet over low heat. One at a time, soak 2 pieces of Ezekiel bread in the egg mixture and place in the skillet. Cook, turning once, until cooked through and golden brown. Serve with maple syrup.

Lunch

Pizza: 2 slices of pizza and broccoli. I love Against the Grain gluten-free frozen pizza, and I promise you will, too, as a healthy alternative.

Dinner

Shrimp and Rice: Sauté chopped red pepper and onion in olive oil, garlic, and lime juice. Add 6 shrimp and sauté until cooked through. Serve with rice.

TUESDAY

Breakfast
Granola with almond milk

Lunch
Quinoa: Combine cooked quinoa with chopped red and yellow bell peppers, black beans, and corn. Add salsa.

Dinner
Turkey Burger: Turkey burger, ½ avocado, asparagus and capers sautéed in olive oil, and 1 cup cooked Pow! pasta with some olive oil and sea salt.

WEDNESDAY

Breakfast
Egg Taco: Scramble 2 eggs and then set them aside on a plate. In the same skillet, heat 1 corn tortilla over low heat. Sprinkle the tortilla with shredded cheese, top with the eggs, and add some more cheese over the eggs. Cover with another tortilla. Turn and cook until the cheese is melted and the bottom is golden.

Lunch
Salad Bowl: Combine fresh baby kale, 1 chopped apple, almonds, and 1 chopped string cheese. Drizzle with dressing of choice.

Dinner
Grilled fish with Pow! pasta with butter, Parmesan, and asparagus tips

THURSDAY

Breakfast
Avocado Toast: Toast
2 slices of Ezekiel bread.
In a small bowl, mash
up 1 avocado with salt
and pepper. Spread over
the toast.

Lunch
**Chopped Salad with
Salmon:** Combine
chopped romaine, cherry
tomatoes, chopped
cucumbers, and grated
Parmesan cheese. Top with
grilled salmon.

Dinner
**Baked chicken with a
sweet potato and green
beans**

FRIDAY

Breakfast
Cereal (choose one of my
favorite picks on page
178) with rice milk, almond
milk, or organic whole milk

Lunch
Tuna Salad: Drain tuna
and put in a bowl. Mix
with 1 tablespoon of
Vegenaise, a squeeze of
yellow mustard, and dill
relish. Spread on 2 slices
of Ezekiel bread.

Dinner
**Pow! Pasta with Your
Favorite Tomato Sauce:**
Cook the pasta according
to package directions.
Drain and return to the
saucepan. Stir in the
tomato sauce and fresh
sliced mozzarella and
reheat.

SATURDAY

Breakfast
Omelet: Make an omelet with 3 eggs, shredded cheese, and chopped avocado. Serve with a side of cherry tomatoes sautéed in avocado oil with rosemary sea salt.

Lunch
Spinach salad: Fresh spinach, red onion, and sweet peas (you can heat frozen peas and then chill them). Add your choice of dressing.

1 apple with almond butter

Dinner
Grilled fish with lemon and rosemary

Crunchy Black Bean Salad: Heat up a can of black beans and then chill them. Chop 1 red pepper, 1 yellow pepper, and 1 rib of celery. Combine in a bowl and then mix in the black beans, crumbled feta cheese, and black olives (if desired). Toss with olive oil and vinegar or Italian dressing.

SUNDAY

Breakfast
English muffin with cream cheese and banana

Lunch
Caprese Sandwich: 2 slices of Ezekiel bread with sliced fresh mozzarella, fresh basil, olive oil, vinegar, and sea salt

Dinner
Grilled Fish with a Side of Asparagus and Easy Mashed Potatoes: Chop and boil 1 large potato. Blend with a hand mixer along with 2 tablespoons of butter and some salt. You can add garlic, too. Serve with the fish and asparagus.

The last week is for when you feel like you have more time to explore in the kitchen. My dear friend and chef Emery Chapman has laid out a week of recipes using whole ingredients that support your health. Following these recipes will teach you how to be savvy in the kitchen.

MONDAY

Breakfast

YOGURT PARFAIT with Fresh Berries and Mint

1 cup organic unsweetened plain yogurt or coconut yogurt	½ cup organic fresh blueberries	2 tablespoons organic fresh mint, chopped
	½ cup organic fresh raspberries	1 tablespoon organic flaxseeds

In a glass, alternately layer the yogurt, blueberries, raspberries, mint, and flaxseeds. Serve immediately.

Lunch

TURKEY AND ROMAINE LETTUCE ROLL-UPS
with Fresh Basil, Avocado, and Tomatoes

4 organic romaine lettuce leaves	4 slices organic smoked turkey breast	½ organic tomato, sliced
		Pinch of sea salt
2 tablespoons organic avocado mayonnaise	3 tablespoons organic basil, torn	Freshly ground black pepper

Using a spatula, spread each romaine lettuce leaf with avocado mayo. Then layer each with some of the turkey, basil, and tomato. Sprinkle with salt and pepper. Serve immediately.

ASIAN-STYLE STIR-FRIED VEGETABLES
with Wild Rice and Pickled Ginger

2 cups filtered water

1 cup organic wild rice

1 cup organic basmati rice

½ cup organic low-sodium, gluten-free tamari

1 tablespoon local raw honey

1 tablespoon organic coconut oil

1 organic yellow onion, chopped

3 tablespoons chopped organic fresh garlic

2 tablespoons peeled and chopped organic fresh ginger

3 tablespoons chopped organic basil

2 heads organic broccoli, stems removed, washed, and cut

1 bunch organic kale

Pinch of sea salt

Freshly ground black pepper

1 jar organic pickled ginger

1. In a medium saucepan, add the water and bring to a boil with the lid on. Add the wild and basmati rices, stir with a spoon, and reduce the heat to low. Simmer, covered, for 30 to 35 minutes, or until the rice is tender. Fluff with a fork and set aside. (If using a rice cooker, simply place the rice and water into the rice cooker, set to the appropriate setting, and let cook.)

2. In a small bowl, whisk the tamari and honey with a fork and then set aside. Add the oil to a large wok or pot and place over high heat. Once the coconut oil has melted, add the onion. Cook for 8 minutes, or until the onion begins to brown. Add the garlic and ginger. Cook, stirring frequently, for 3 minutes, then add the basil. Add the broccoli and kale and cook for 5 to 8 minutes, or until the broccoli is just tender. Pour the reserved tamari mixture over the vegetables and reduce the heat to low. Season with salt and pepper. Simmer for 5 minutes so that all the flavors can come together.

3. Put the rice in a bowl, then top with the veggies and sauce. You can add additional tamari and garnish with pickled ginger, if desired.

TUESDAY

Breakfast

CHOCOLATE PROTEIN SMOOTHIE
with Blueberries, Cinnamon, and
Frozen Coconut

1 cup filtered water

2 scoops chocolate
protein powder (I
recommend Tera's Whey
Organic Protein Powder!)

1 cup frozen organic
blueberries

1 package (8 ounces)
frozen coconut (or
8 ounces fresh coconut
water with some ice; I like
Harmless Harvest)

1 teaspoon ground
Ceylon cinnamon

In a blender, combine the water, protein powder, blueberries, coconut, and cinnamon.
Blend on high until all of the ingredients are fully combined. Drink immediately.

SLICED TOMATO
with Fresh Basil, Romaine Lettuce, and Walnut Pâté

WALNUT PÂTÉ*

1½ cups raw walnuts

1 tablespoon olive oil

2 small shallots, finely chopped

1 clove garlic, minced

2 tablespoons finely chopped scallions

Sea salt

Freshly ground black pepper

2 tablespoons gluten-free tamari

¼ cup water

3 organic romaine lettuce leaves

1 organic tomato, cored and sliced

3 tablespoons organic fresh basil, torn

1. Place the walnuts in a medium bowl and fill the bowl with cool water. Soak for at least 2 hours.

2. In a large skillet, heat the oil over medium heat. Add the shallots, garlic, scallions, and salt and pepper to taste. Cook, stirring frequently, for 8 minutes, or until the shallots are golden brown. Set aside.

3. Drain the soaked walnuts and transfer to a food processor. Add the reserved shallot mixture and the tamari. Pulse the mixture until it begins to combine. Slowly add the water until the mixture becomes smooth (up to ¼ cup of water).

4. Arrange the lettuce leaves on a plate. Layer the tomato slices with the walnut pâté and fresh basil until all of the tomato slices are gone. Place over the lettuce and enjoy!

***CHEF'S NOTE:** The walnut pâté can be made in advance and stored in an airtight container for up to 7 days. It is great as a snack with cucumber slices or any type of sliced veggie. It also makes a fantastic sandwich spread.

Dinner

GLUTEN-FREE QUESADILLA with Fresh Spinach, Refried Beans, and Monterey Jack Cheese

2 gluten-free tortillas

¼ can (15.4 ounces) organic refried beans

½ cup organic spinach

¼ package (8 ounces) organic Monterey Jack cheese, shredded

½ tablespoon organic olive oil

¼ jar (16 ounces) organic salsa

1. Place 1 tortilla on a plate. Using a spatula, spread some of the refried beans evenly over the tortilla. Then sprinkle with the spinach and cheese.

2. Place the second tortilla on top, making a sandwich. In a large skillet, heat the oil over medium heat. Add the quesadilla and cook for 10 minutes, turning once, or until golden brown. Cut the quesadilla into slices and serve with the salsa. You can also serve with a big salad, hot sauce, guacamole, fresh lime wedges, or cilantro, just to name a few ideas.

WEDNESDAY

Breakfast

SCRAMBLED EGGS with Sautéed Onion, Fresh Parsley, and Tomatoes

2 organic eggs

1 tablespoon organic grass-fed butter, coconut oil, ghee, or olive oil (your choice)

3 tablespoons finely chopped organic onion

6–8 organic whole cherry tomatoes

3 tablespoons chopped organic fresh parsley

Pinch of sea salt

Freshly ground black pepper

1. Crack the eggs into a small bowl and whisk with a fork. Set aside.

2. In a small skillet, heat the butter or oil over medium heat. Add the onion and cook for 8 minutes, or until golden brown. Add the tomatoes, parsley, and salt and pepper to taste. Cook for 2 minutes. Pour the reserved eggs over the vegetables. Cook, stirring slowly with a wooden spoon, for 5 minutes, or until just cooked through. Serve immediately.

TUNA SALAD with Capers and Red Onion on a Bed of Greens

1 can (5 ounces) wild-caught yellowfin tuna, drained

3 tablespoons organic capers

2 tablespoons finely chopped organic red onion

1 tablespoon finely chopped organic fresh parsley

3 tablespoons fresh organic lemon juice

2 tablespoons organic avocado mayonnaise

Pinch of sea salt

Freshly ground black pepper

2 cups organic mixed greens

1. In a medium bowl, add the tuna and flake with a fork. Add the capers, onion, parsley, lemon juice, avocado mayo, and salt and pepper to taste. Use your fork to fully combine all of the ingredients.

2. Arrange the mixed greens on top of a plate. Top with the tuna salad. If desired, add additional ground black pepper and freshly squeezed lemon juice.

Dinner

MARINATED GRILLED CHICKEN SANDWICH
with Red Onion and Avocado Slices

¼ cup organic apple cider vinegar

¼ cup organic olive oil

1 teaspoon sea salt

Freshly ground black pepper

1 tablespoon organic dried oregano

1 tablespoon organic real maple syrup

1 organic boneless, skinless chicken breast half

1 organic gluten-free sandwich bun

Organic romaine lettuce leaves

Organic tomato slices

Organic red onion slices

Organic avocado slices

1. In a glass container, combine the vinegar, oil, salt, pepper to taste, oregano, and maple syrup. Whisk with a fork. Add the chicken to the marinade and turn to coat. Marinate in the refrigerator for 30 minutes to 1 hour.

2. Preheat a grill to high or heat a large skillet over high heat. Remove the chicken from the marinade and grill or cook for 16 minutes, turning once, or until a thermometer inserted in the thickest portion registers 165°F and the juices run clear.

3. Place the chicken on the bun. Add lettuce and sliced tomato, onion, and avocado as desired. You could also add ketchup, mustard, avocado mayo, pickles, microgreens, or lacto-fermented dill pickle sauerkraut, just to name a few options. Whatever your favorite combination is!

THURSDAY

Breakfast

GLUTEN-FREE OATMEAL with Chia Seeds, Tamari Almonds, and Fresh Blueberries

1 cup organic gluten-free oatmeal

1 cup water or organic nut milk

1 tablespoon organic chia seeds

1 teaspoon ground Ceylon cinnamon

Pinch of sea salt

2 tablespoons gluten-free tamari almonds

½ cup organic fresh blueberries

In a small pot, combine the oatmeal, water or nut milk, chia seeds, cinnamon, and salt. Place the pot over medium heat and bring the oatmeal to a boil. Reduce the heat to low and cook for 3 minutes, or until desired consistency. Remove from the heat and transfer the oatmeal to your favorite bowl. Garnish with the almonds and blueberries. Enjoy!

GLUTEN-FREE WRAP FILLED
with Hummus, Fresh Herbs, and Tomatoes

1 gluten-free wrap

3 tablespoons organic hummus

3 tablespoons organic lacto-fermented dill pickle sauerkraut (optional)

1 tablespoon chopped organic fresh dill

1 tablespoon chopped organic fresh basil

1 tablespoon chopped organic fresh cilantro

½ organic tomato, sliced

Place the wrap on a plate. Using a spatula, spread the hummus evenly in the center of the wrap. Add the sauerkraut (if desired), dill, basil, and cilantro. Add the tomato slices and fold the bottom edge of the wrap up. Roll the wrap up and eat immediately.

Dinner

CHICKEN COCONUT CURRY

1 pound organic boneless, skinless chicken breast halves, chopped

2 cloves organic garlic, sliced

3 tablespoons chopped organic fresh cilantro

2 organic scallions, chopped

4 tablespoons fish sauce, divided

1 tablespoon organic olive oil

1 teaspoon sea salt

Freshly ground black pepper

1 teaspoon organic coconut oil

½ teaspoon mild yellow curry powder

1 large head organic broccoli, stems removed, chopped

3 tablespoons chopped organic fresh basil

1 can (13.5 ounces) organic full-fat coconut milk

2 tablespoons organic real maple syrup

Cooked rice (optional)

1. In a bowl, combine the chicken, garlic, cilantro, scallions, 2 tablespoons of the fish sauce, olive oil, salt, and pepper to taste. Marinate in the refrigerator for 1 hour.

2. In a large wok or skillet over high heat, heat the coconut oil. Once the coconut oil is melted, add the chicken and cook for 6 to 8 minutes, or until the chicken is firm. Add the curry powder and cook for 1 minute. Add the broccoli and basil and cook for 1 minute. Stir in the coconut milk, maple syrup, and remaining 2 tablespoons fish sauce. Reduce the heat to low and simmer for 5 minutes, or until the broccoli is just tender. Serve with rice or on its own.

FRIDAY

DARK CHERRY AND BANANA SMOOTHIE

1 cup filtered water	**½ cup frozen organic dark cherries**
2 scoops protein powder	
½ frozen organic banana	**2 tablespoons organic flaxseeds**

In a blender, combine the water, protein powder, banana, cherries, and flaxseeds. Blend on high speed for 1 minute, or until all of the ingredients are fully combined. Drink immediately.

Lunch

GLUTEN-FREE AVOCADO TOAST
with Fried Eggs

2 slices gluten-free bread

½ organic avocado, halved and pitted

Pinch of sea salt

Freshly ground black pepper

1 tablespoon organic grass-fed butter, ghee, olive oil, or coconut oil

2 organic eggs

Handful of microgreens (optional)

1. In a toaster, toast the bread. Place the toast on a plate. Using a spoon, scoop the avocado out of the peel and spread on each piece of toast. Sprinkle with salt and pepper to taste and set aside.

2. In a small skillet, heat the butter or oil over medium heat. Once the butter or oil is melted, crack both of the eggs into the pan. Cook for 6 to 8 minutes, or until cooked to desired doneness. Using a spatula, remove the eggs from the pan and place on top of the avocado toast. Sprinkle with microgreens if you like and eat immediately.

POLENTA with Roasted Vegetables

1 pint organic cherry tomatoes

1 organic onion, sliced

1 organic shallot, sliced

¼ cup chopped organic fresh basil

1 tablespoon organic fresh thyme

2 tablespoons organic olive oil

1 pinch + 1 teaspoon sea salt

Freshly ground black pepper

1 quart (4 cups) filtered water

2 cups organic polenta

2 tablespoons organic grass-fed butter

2 tablespoons grated organic Parmesan cheese, plus additional for garnish

1. Preheat the oven to 450°F. On a large sheet pan, combine the tomatoes, onion, and shallot. Sprinkle with the basil, thyme, oil, a pinch of the salt, and pepper to taste. Roast for 30 minutes, or until the vegetables are tender and browned.

2. Meanwhile, add the water to a medium saucepan, cover, and bring to a boil over high heat. Once boiling, add the polenta, the remaining 1 teaspoon salt, and pepper to taste. Cover the pot and reduce the heat to low. Cook for 30 to 35 minutes, or until nearly all of the liquid is absorbed. Remove from the heat. Fluff with a fork and add the butter and cheese.

3. Spoon a portion of the polenta onto a plate. Add a portion of the roasted vegetables over the top. Garnish with additional freshly ground black pepper and cheese, if desired. Serve immediately.

SATURDAY

Breakfast

GLUTEN-FREE BLUEBERRY PANCAKES

2 organic eggs

2 cups organic nut milk or buttermilk

2 tablespoons organic olive oil

1 teaspoon sea salt

1 teaspoon ground Ceylon cinnamon

1 teaspoon vanilla extract

2 cups gluten-free flour (I recommend Pamela's Baking Mix)

1 cup organic blueberries + additional for serving

Organic grass-fed butter

Organic real maple syrup

1. Into a large bowl, crack the eggs. Add the milk, oil, salt, cinnamon, and vanilla. Whisk with a fork until fully combined. Add the flour and whisk until fully combined. Add the blueberries and gently fold them into the batter with your fork until distributed evenly.

2. Heat a griddle or large skillet over medium heat. Add 1 tablespoon of butter and cook until melted. Spoon the batter into the skillet, making individual pancakes. Cook for 2 to 4 minutes, or until bubbles begin to form on the top. Turn and cook for 2 to 4 minutes, or until fully cooked through and golden brown on the bottom. Repeat with additional butter and batter until all of the batter has been used. Serve immediately with a touch of butter, maple syrup, and more fresh blueberries.

Lunch

QUINOA SALAD with Cucumber, Feta Cheese, Olives, Red Pepper, and Pumpkin Seeds

2 cups filtered water

2 cups sprouted organic quinoa

½ cup organic olive oil

½ cup organic apple cider vinegar

1 teaspoon sea salt

Freshly ground black pepper

1 tablespoon organic dried oregano

1 tablespoon organic real maple syrup

1 organic red pepper, chopped

1 organic cucumber, peeled and chopped

1 cup pitted organic kalamata olives

¼ cup cubed organic feta cheese

¼ cup raw organic pumpkin seeds

3 tablespoons chopped organic fresh basil

3 tablespoons chopped organic fresh mint

1. Add the water to a medium saucepan, cover, and bring to a boil. Stir in the quinoa, cover, reduce the heat to low, and cook for 30 to 35 minutes, or until all of the liquid has been absorbed. Alternately, you can place the water and quinoa in a rice cooker and set to the appropriate setting. Once cooked, fluff with a fork and set aside.

2. Meanwhile, in a small bowl, combine the oil, vinegar, salt, black pepper to taste, oregano, and maple syrup. Whisk with a fork and set aside.

3. Transfer the quinoa to a large bowl. Add the red pepper, cucumber, olives, cheese, pumpkin seeds, basil, and mint. Whisk the dressing one last time and pour over the quinoa mixture. Toss well and serve immediately. The vegetables, fresh herbs, and seeds or nuts can be altered for this dish.

CURRIED BUTTERNUT SQUASH AND CARROT SOUP

2 tablespoons organic olive oil

½ organic onion, chopped

1 teaspoon sea salt

Freshly ground black pepper

2 tablespoons mild curry powder

1 clove organic garlic, minced

1 medium organic butternut squash, halved, seeded, peeled, and chopped

2 organic carrots, chopped

3 cups low-sodium organic vegetable or chicken stock

1. In a large stockpot, heat the oil over medium heat. Add the onion, salt, and pepper to taste and cook for 8 minutes, or until the onion is tender. Stir in the curry powder and garlic and cook for 1 minute. Add the butternut squash and carrots and cook for 5 minutes, stirring continuously so the vegetables don't burn. Add the stock, cover, and bring almost to a boil. Reduce the heat to low and cook for 20 minutes, or until all of the vegetables are tender. Pour the soup into a blender. Place the lid on the blender, making sure it is firmly in place, and start blending on medium speed. Gradually increase to high speed and blend until the soup becomes smooth. Return to the pot and heat through over low heat.

2. Spoon the soup into bowls and garnish with fresh herbs, black pepper, pumpkin seeds, and a touch of sour cream or coconut yogurt, if desired. You can also serve this with gluten-free toast points.

Breakfast

MINI CRUSTLESS QUICHES

2 tablespoons organic olive oil	¼ cup chopped organic fresh basil	2 cups organic fresh spinach
½ organic onion, chopped	Pinch of sea salt	1 dozen organic eggs
½ organic red pepper, chopped	Freshly ground black pepper	1 cup organic buttermilk or milk

1. Preheat the oven to 350°F. Using your hands, grease a 12-cup muffin pan with olive oil or cooking spray.

2. In a large skillet, heat the oil over medium heat. Add the onion, red pepper, basil, and salt and black pepper to taste. Cook for 8 minutes, or until the veggies are tender. Add the spinach and cook for 2 to 4 minutes, or until it just begins to wilt. Remove from the heat and set aside.

3. Into a medium bowl, crack the eggs. Add the milk and whisk well with a fork. Using a spoon, divide the reserved vegetables evenly among the muffin cups. Pour the egg mixture over the vegetables until all 12 muffin cups are filled. Bake for 25 to 30 minutes, or until the eggs are firm. Remove from the oven and let stand for 5 minutes before removing from the pan. Serve immediately. These can be stored in an airtight container for 4 to 5 days for a quick, easy, and healthy breakfast.

Lunch

GRILLED PORTOBELLO MUSHROOM SANDWICH
with Hummus and Microgreens

2 organic portobello mushroom caps

1 tablespoon organic olive oil

2 tablespoons organic balsamic vinegar

Pinch of sea salt

Freshly ground black pepper

¼ cup organic hummus

1 cup organic microgreens

1 wedge lemon (optional)

1. Wash the mushroom caps and place in a dish. Drizzle the mushrooms with the oil and vinegar and season to taste with the salt and pepper. Let marinate for 5 to 10 minutes. Preheat a grill or skillet to high heat. Add the mushrooms with the marinade and cook for 10 to 16 minutes, turning once, or until tender.

2. Place a mushroom cap on a plate. Using a spatula, evenly spread the hummus over the mushroom. Top with the microgreens and then place the second mushroom cap on top, making a sandwich. Squeeze the lemon wedge over the top, if desired. Serve immediately.

GLUTEN-FREE PESTO PASTA with Roasted Cauliflower

1 head organic cauliflower, cut into florets

2 tablespoons organic olive oil

2 tablespoons chopped organic fresh parsley

1 teaspoon sea salt

Freshly ground black pepper

PESTO

2 cups organic fresh basil leaves

½ cup organic pine nuts

½ cup grated organic Parmesan cheese

¼ cup organic olive oil

1 teaspoon sea salt

Freshly ground black pepper

1 package (12 ounces) gluten-free spaghetti

1. Preheat the oven to 425°F. In a large sheet pan, spread out the cauliflower pieces evenly. Drizzle with the oil and sprinkle with the parsley. Season with the salt and pepper to taste. Roast for 25 to 30 minutes, or until the cauliflower is golden brown. Remove from the oven and set aside.

2. **To make the pesto:** In a food processor or blender, combine the basil, pine nuts, cheese, oil, salt, and pepper to taste. Process or blend on high speed. If the mixture is too thick, add 1 to 2 tablespoons of water to thin it. Once the pesto is fully combined, use a spatula to transfer it to a glass container with a lid. Set aside.

3. Prepare the pasta to al dente according to package directions. Drain and return to the pot. Add 2 to 3 tablespoons of the pesto to the pasta and toss until the pasta is just fully combined with the pesto. If your pasta looks dry, add another tablespoon of pesto until it's fully cooked. Any remaining pesto can be stored in your fridge to be used as a sandwich spread, or you can freeze it for another time.

4. Spoon a portion of the pesto noodles onto a plate and top with some of the roasted cauliflower. Save any leftovers for another meal, or share with your family or a friend!

5. Garnish with additional fresh parsley, Parmesan cheese, and black pepper to your liking. It is even delicious with a small squeeze of lemon juice. Serve immediately.

VOCABULARY

ARABESQUE: straight leg position reaching back or up toward the ceiling with knee facing side

ATTITUDE: leg is raised back in a 90-degree angle bent position with knee to the side

BRIDGE: an upside-down plank with bent knees

COUPÉ: bend the knee and touch either the opposite ankle or the back of the knee

CROSSED ARABESQUE: leg is crossed behind body toward opposite side instead of straight back

DOWN DOG HIPS: body is in an upside-down V position with hands and feet on floor and hips up high

FOURTH POSITION: leg crossed back behind opposite shoulder on floor and bent

HIP DIP: lower hip toward floor without lowering all the way down

HIP SIT: place hip down to floor

HIP TAP: quickly touch hip to floor and lift without placing weight fully down

HOVER: slightly lifted off floor

HYDRANT: leg is pulled forward toward shoulder in an attitude position when kneeling on knees

INVERTED KNEE TAP: knee turns in toward opposite knee and gently touches the floor

NONWORKING ARM/LEG: the arm or leg that is supporting the body and not moving

OPEN DIAGONAL: leg is open slightly side/back instead of straight back

PARALLEL ARABESQUE: straight leg arabesque with knee facing down

PASSÉ: knee is bent with toes touching opposite inner knee

PLANK: hands down with wrists directly under shoulders and arms straight, feet down with straight legs hip width apart

PLIÉ: bend the knees and straighten

WIDE PLANK: plank position with feet wider than shoulders

WORKING ARM/LEG: the arm or leg doing the action

First, I would like to dedicate this book to my parents, Diana Jean Blythe and Robert Scott Richardson. A few of my favorite things they taught me that I have kept dear to me in raising my kids are "You are unique in this world. You must always honor that" and "You aren't better than anyone, and no one is better than you." And what Thumper said, "If you can't say something nice, don't say anything at all." As my mother would add, "That includes the way you speak to yourself." She taught me to feel confident in my own skin, and my father taught me to be limitless in my mental capacity as a young woman. They encouraged me to take all that I was capable of and put everything I had into it. They believed.

To my son, Sam Anderson, who is off to his first year in college, as this book is being released. He is a big-hearted big brother, an inspiring artist, and a thoughtful leader and friend. And to my daughter, Penelope Blythe Mogol, who is the most spirited sweetheart. A dancer and a dream catcher with a smile that can light up the universe.

I would like to thank the beautiful and talented Ava Lantiere and Isabella Dirussa for being a part of my book.

I would not have been able to write this book that meant so very much to me to bring forward for teens if it weren't for my incredible team. The indispensable Steven Beltrani, whose courage, intelligence, loyalty, pure heart, and ability to lead with the clearest communication makes it possible for me to support my audience at large.

My dear friend, the supremely talented iconic author Lise Erin, for being there for me as a writer that I needed to lean into to be able to make this book possible.

My writer, Marisa Belger, for being so tolerant, like-minded, and thoughtful in her approach to collaborating.

A super special thank you to my sweet assistant, Meg Schiavoni, who I couldn't juggle even two balls in the air let alone 50 without; the very talented and keen-eyed Aja Marie Johnson; the super human superstar stylist Karyn Shapiro, who has dressed me for 15 years; the most enchanting makeup artist and fine oil maker LeAnne Hirsh; and my hair goddess and dear pal, the super talented Korey Fitzpatrick.

A special dedication to chef Emery Chapman for fighting the good food fight for the health of our children's futures. Thank you for supporting me with your amazing chef skills to make healthy feel as yummy as ever.

A special thank you to Susan Blacklocke from Provisions organic food market in Sag Harbor, NY, for your tips and tricks.

The biggest most heartfelt thank you to my awesome, patient, and big-hearted agent Steve Troha, and to the entire Rodale team. I have never been more impressed by a team.

Ignite your muscles. Clear your mind. Fuel your body.

ACKNOWLEDGMENTS

INDEX

Underscored page references indicate boxed text.

Tea, 179
Technology, physical
        inactivity linked to,
        48–49
Teeth, brushing, 47–48
Temple, body compared to,
        5
Thankfulness, 17, 19
Thoughts
    inventory of, 9
    negative, 11–12
    noticing, 9
Tiredness, 6
Total body workouts, 52
Tuna Salad, 187, 196
Twist Roll to Tap, 152

U

Unhealthy food habits,
        breaking, 22–24,
        26–27
Uniqueness, appreciating,
        2–3
Urban Drill workout
    Arabesque to Attitude,
        82
    Arms Down, Heels Up,
        77
    Do the Twist, 78
    Fifth Position High/Low,
        79
    Hydrant Pull to Side
        Kick, 81
    Legs Up, Bent Crunch,
        88
    Plank Reaches, 85
    Side Plank to Kick Front,
        84
    Stacked Legs to
        Arabesque, 80
    Wide Down Dog Reach,
        86
    Wide V Swipe Cross
        Open, 89
    Wide V Tap, Extend Up,
        90

V

Vanishing caloric density, 31
Vegetables
    Asian-Style Stir-Fried
        Vegetables with
        Wild Rice and
        Pickled Ginger, 191
    Asparagus Omelet, 184
    Avocado Toast, 187
    Chopped Salad, 182, 183
    Chopped Salad with
        Salmon, 187
    Curried Butternut
        Squash and Carrot
        Soup, 206
    dirty dozen list, 33
    Gluten-Free Avocado
        Toast with Fried
        Eggs, 202
    Grilled Portobello
        Mushroom
        Sandwich with
        Hummus and
        Microgreens, 208
    Mini Crustless Quiches,
        207
    organic foods, 32–35
    Polenta with Roasted
        Vegetables, 203
    Salad Bowl, 186
    salads, 179
    Sliced Tomato with Fresh
        Basil, Romaine
        Lettuce, and Walnut
        Pâté, 193
    Spinach Salad with
        Fresh Spinach, Red
        Onion, and Sweet
        Peas, 188
    washing, 179
Vehicle, body compared to, 6

W

Walnut Pâté, 193
W Arms, 95

Weight fluctuations, 41
Weight gain during college,
        xi
Weight loss
    extreme dieting, 45–46
    movement fundamental
        to, 46
    starting from within, 4
Whole foods
    benefits of, 31–32
    for breakfast, 37
    general discussion,
        28–29
    vs. processed foods,
        29–31, 29
    switching to, 40
Wide Down Dog Reach, 86
Wide plank, defined, 210
Wide Plank Crossed Knee
        Pulls, 173
Wide V Swipe Cross Open,
        89
Wide V Tap, Extend Up, 90
Wild-caught fish, 35
Working arm/leg, defined,
        210
Working Heel Stretch, 139
Working out. *See also*
        specific exercises;
        specific workouts
    benefits of, 46, 48
    curiosity and awareness
        in, 54–55, 57
    daily, 47, 47, 50, 56
    disconnection from body,
        44–46
    five things to practice, 56
    focused movement,
        52–54
    integrating in everyday
        life, 47–49, 56
    mind and body in, 52
    music for, 53, 56
    scheduling workouts, 50
    vs. sports, 49–50
Worries, 8, 9
Wrap Back Attitude, 68
Writing. *See* Journaling

JAN – – 2018